LYNDON B. JOHNSON

A MEMOIR

LYNDON B. JOHNSON
A MEMOIR

by George Reedy

ANDREWS AND MC MEEL, INC.
A Universal Press Syndicate Company
NEW YORK • KANSAS CITY

Library of Congress Cataloging in Publication Data

Reedy, George E., 1917 –
   Lyndon B. Johnson, a memoir

   1. Johnson, Lyndon B. (Lyndon Baines), 1908–1973.
2. United States—Politics and government—1945–
3. Presidents—United States—Biography. I. Title.
E847.R36   1982   973.923'092'4 [B]   82-13739

ISBN 0-8362-6610-2

First Printing, September 1982
Second Printing, January 1983

Acknowledgments

Although this book is a personal production, I owe debts of gratitude which must be acknowledged. First, there is James F. Scotton, dean of journalism at Marquette, who read the manuscript and saved me from much of the prolixity to which I am unfortunately addicted. Then there is Zoe Smith, my faculty colleague, who produced for the cover a picture of me that is kindly without being overflattering and realistic without being overly dull.

There are many colleagues who worked with me during the crucial years for whom I cherish the warmest of memories. I do not believe I need name names. There are friendships which truly last.

Finally, there is my wife, who did the proofreading which is essential to any author and at which I am not very good. What should really be said, however, is that she deserves not only thanks but heavenly reward for the years she spent holding the family together with love and tenderness while I was living in the orbit of the man described in this book. Job never had such patience nor Penelope such faithfulness. I am grateful.

GEORGE E. REEDY

Contents

Foreword

It took me many wasted years to realize that this is a book I had to write — not for the rest of the world but for myself. This is not an effort at history, biography, or political analysis even though all three intellectual disciplines are involved. They enter only insofar as they give coherence to my own thoughts. The real key to what follows is the effort to rearrange memories of an experience so they become understandable to me and therefore livable.

The word "livable" is very important. This book is not about Lyndon B. Johnson but about my reactions to Lyndon B. Johnson. For nearly two decades, he was the physically dominant force in my life. What I discovered after leaving him was that geographical, social, and political separation did not put an end to his presence. Even dead, he remained a force. What is happening here is an effort to get some things off my chest. In a very real sense, this is an exercise in exorcism.

Why I went to work for him was a mystery to most of my friends. They had known me as a Socialist in my younger days — the president of the University of Chicago Socialist Club and the editor of a student magazine called *Soapbox*. Those who knew my family also knew that I was descended from fire-eating abolitionists — potato-famine Irish who looked upon the slave holders of the South as American counterparts of the Sassenachs who had made life so miserable for them in their homeland. To find me transferring overnight from journalist to staff aide for a Texas senator was, to them, bewildering.

It was even more difficult for them to understand why I continued to work for the man after I had been with him long enough to have the full flavor. He was notorious for abusing his staff, for driving people to the verge of exhaustion — and sometimes over the verge; for paying the lowest salaries for the longest hours of work on Capitol Hill; for publicly humiliating his most loyal aides; for keeping his office in a constant state of turmoil by playing games with reigning male and female favorites.

There was no sense in which he could be described as a pleasant man. His manners were atrocious — not just slovenly but frequently *calculated* to give offense. Relaxation was something he did not understand and would not accord to others. He was a bully who would exercise merciless sarcasm on people who could not fight back but could only take it. Most important, he had no sense of loyalty — at least, not the kind of loyalty I learned on the Irish Near North Side of Chicago, where life was bearable only because people who had very little in the way of worldly goods had very much in the way of mutual trust. To Johnson, loyalty was a one-way street: all take on his part and all give on the part of everyone else — his family, his friends, his supporters.

Under the circumstances, a number of mythologies took root among those who had known me before I joined the LBJ entourage. Most of them centered around the idea that I *knew* he was going to be president someday. When I became press secretary of the White House, stories appeared quoting me as having once said: "I am hitching my wagon to a star!"

If I ever said anything like that, I must have been fried to the gills. I realized that he *might* be president and I thought that he *should* be president but I was skeptical that he would ever achieve that status. In the early fifties — the years we are now discussing — the split in the Democratic Party was so deep that prospects were remote for the nomination to go to anyone from a Confederate state. The Democratic Party was star-studded with liberals — names such as Harriman, Kefauver, Stevenson, Symington — and it was obvious that other stars (such as Kennedy) were just over the horizon. They swung relatively little weight in the Congress, but there was no doubt of their predominant influence in the machinery that selected presiden-

tial candidates. That machinery was not going to accord the top spot
on a Democratic ticket to any Southerner with the possible exception
of Estes Kefauver, who had mastered the fine art of keeping at least
three paces to the left of all of his colleagues.

There was another problem even more difficult than that of the
North-South split. The liberal politicians of that era had discovered
that of all their crusades, the most popular was their opposition to the
oil industry. The petroleum barons were an excellent target. Their
wealth was beyond belief. They were possessed of the arrogance that
always characterizes a new elite. Many of them had gone from rags to
riches by a lucky "strike" and some of them were crude, uneducated,
and lacking the wisdom of the older affluent families in the East who
had learned to avoid public displays of their money. The industry not
only bought and sold politicians but bragged about its acquisitions. A
huge financial empire had been built on the hydrocarbons laid under
the soil millions of years ago, and its political center was Texas. In the
eyes of people in the non-oil-producing areas, every politician in the
state — even the sainted Sam Rayburn — was spattered to varying
degrees by oil and the senators were regarded as drenched in the
stuff.

Unfortunately, the political realities of Texas life lent credibility to
charges that its representatives were "owned" by the oil industry
even when those charges were very unfair — as they were in the case
of Lyndon B. Johnson. By a quirk in the state's Constitution, the
production of oil in Texas had been tied to the education of Texas
schoolchildren. This had not been intended by the Populist Governor
Jim Hogg, who had established a commission to break the monopoly
power of the railroads in the early part of this century. The commission had been given power over the revenues from the public lands
which, under another provision of the Constitution, were to be
devoted to education. What this meant to the public was that the
health of the oil industry was considered a measure of the quality of
schooling available to the young. It was not a terribly logical thesis
and could be refuted easily in any intellectual debate. We are not
concerned here with logic or economics, however. The fact remains
that this was the perception of most Texans and it was skillfully
exploited. For a Texas representative to vote "against" the oil industry was the equivalent of a Wisconsin representative voting against
butter, an Idaho representative voting against wool, or a Mississippi
representative voting against cotton. Johnson had to go along even
though in his campaigns he had strongly organized opposition from

most Texas oilmen who thought he was so near to a Communist as to make no difference.

Another problem was the strong suspicion that he had "stolen" his Senate seat. The story of the famous 87 votes from Jim Wells County, which appeared opportunely to win the 1948 race, became legendary to Americans who had never seen the lower Rio Grande Valley and had no idea of the conditions of life in that area. The truth will never be known with any certainty. I am not going to rehash it here, as the situation is far too complicated to explain in a few sentences and is irrelevant to this book. I content myself with asserting that I looked into it as carefully as I could and came to the honest conclusion that Johnson had received the most votes in that campaign and whatever stealing went on had offsets. More important, I am convinced that Johnson himself was innocent of any complicity and the real problem arose from two bosses trying to knife each other in seamy border politics.

My own personal convictions that he had been elected honestly, however, were certainly not enough to eradicate the aura of political rinkydinks that surrounded the Johnson name. Taken together with the civil rights struggle and the ill repute that oil had brought to Texas, it was enough to cast serious doubt on consideration ever being given to an LBJ presidential candidacy.

I was looking at something else. It seemed to me early in 1950 that observers of the Senate were viewing him in the wrong perspective. They were so blinded by his debits on the presidential rating board that they were not looking at his assets on the national political scene. I was looking at those assets and I thought they were considerable.

I had discovered early that the man had a remarkable capacity for persuading people to work together even when they didn't like each other very much. He was equally at home with conservative Richard B. Russell of Georgia and liberal Stuart Symington of Missouri; with Leverett Saltonstall, a Massachusetts Republican, and Warren Magnusson, a Democrat from the other side of the continent. He had established a committee to investigate certain phases of the Korean War and had succeeded in achieving unanimous report after unanimous report on some very controversial subjects. In the turbulent Washington of the early 1950s, these things represented a talent that was virtually lacking in every other quarter.

It was a period in which the government of the United States had come to a standstill. It was possible to sustain routine operations, but badly needed innovations were out of the question. A coalition of

Southern Democrats and conservative Republicans controlled Congress, despite the nominal Democratic majorities, and was blocking all presidential proposals. Paralysis was too strong a word, but there was not much action even though the need for action was plain. Joseph McCarthy had launched his "anti-Communist" crusade, which did not succeed in exposing any previously unexposed Communists but which did take the heart out of the federal bureaucracy. Aside from investigations, Congress seemed helpless to do anything other than approve the routine nominations, and the executive agencies were too cowed to move.

This was the period in which I joined the Johnson staff. I am not quite certain how it happened because he could move fast. But I was quite willing because he appealed to me as the one center of stability in a political world which otherwise had gone berserk. In this respect, I was right. He did, almost single-handedly, pull the pieces back together. He did, almost single-handedly, convert the fractionalized Democratic Senate group into a cohesive whole — a unity which became infectious and spread to other parts of the party. He did, almost single-handedly, restore dignity to the Senate. It was a magnificent performance.

As far as I am concerned, Johnson does deserve a place in a political Hall of Fame for two reasons. First, his leadership in the early fifties, more than anything else, including the election of Dwight D. Eisenhower, put the nation's political machinery back on the track in a period when it was threatening to jump the rails. Second, in the early sixties, when President Kennedy was assassinated, he demonstrated to the American people that a crackpot with a mail-order rifle could not kill the government of the United States. These were two achievements which should overshadow all the programs and legislative triumphs that he himself thought would be his monument in history.

This was really the characteristic that kept many people working for Lyndon B. Johnson through thick and thin. It was not a pleasant life. He was cruel, even to people who had virtually walked the last mile for him. Occasionally he would demonstrate his gratitude for extraordinary services by a lavish gift — an expensive suit of clothes, an automobile, jewelry for the women on his staff. The gift was always followed by an outpouring of irrelevant abuse (I believe he thought his impulse was an example of weakness for which he had to atone) and a few members of his entourage noted that the gift was invariably tax deductible on his part. Furthermore, some of the most lavish presents frequently went to members who had performed no services other than adulation. And when his personal desires were at stake, he had absolutely no consideration for the situation in which other people found themselves. They were required to drop everything to wait upon him and were expected to forget their private lives in his interests. He even begrudged one of his top assistants a telephone call to his wife on their wedding anniversary, which the assistant was spending on the LBJ ranch and his wife at their home in Washington, D.C.

Gratitude was not his strongest suit. When he entered the White House, he was obsessed by a desire to be surrounded by young people. He even ordered me to fire one of the older and more competent assistants who had lived for years with no dedication other than to Lyndon B. Johnson. I flatly refused and got away with it because even he had too much sense to get into a public row with anyone as visible as the White House press secretary. But it was one of the incidents — and they kept growing — which eventually led to our split.

Time after time, these conditions of life led me and many others to the beginning stages of resignation. But each time, he would do something so magnificent that all of his nasty characteristics would fade. I was ready to quit in 1956 when — in a display of extremely high political courage — he met Allan Shivers in a head-on clash to decide whether the Democratic Party of Texas would be a sham front for conservative Republicans to use in taking over the state or whether it would give the voters an honest choice. I could not desert him in that kind of contest and I forgot my grievances. I almost quit in 1957 but he decided that the time was ripe to tackle the civil rights issue and, again, I could not leave. Most of my life with him was like that — from the days when he decided the forces were finally ripe to censure McCarthy to the night in New Orleans in 1964 when he publicly chided Southerners for their treatment of blacks — and drew applause that is still ringing in my ears. He could be superb!

In retrospect, I do not regret the years I spent with him — however agonizing. He was a tormented man, and I realize now that this was so much a part of his being that he had to lash out even at people he loved. I do not know why he was tormented although I can make some guesses, and I will set them forth in the coming pages. Here, I will only say that the painful memories are tempered by what I learned. Basically, he proved to me — and I hope to others — that the system really does work if only it is taken for what it is rather than for what we think it ought to be. Stated that way, it seems like an obvious doctrine. It is not at all obvious, however, to the model builders who dominate most contemporary political analysis and who leave out of their models the interaction between political forces and political leaders.

This was a point that Johnson understood thoroughly. He knew — and he often stated — that leaders could not accomplish anything without troops. He was very fond of a Texas saying: "Don't try to kill the snake unless you've got the hoe in your hands." He did not move until he had that hoe and his refusal was often — and mistakenly — attributed to cowardice. Politically, he had as much courage as any man I have ever known. He merely refused to engage an enemy in battle until he had the forces deployed. The censure of McCarthy came when his plans for lining up the necessary votes had matured. His successful effort to push a civil rights bill through Congress came after he was convinced that there was a winning balance of power. He thought windmills were made for electric power rather than tilting targets.

What is in these pages will not be greeted with pleasure by those who regard themselves as the custodians of the Lyndon Johnson legend. The effort to "civilize" him in the eyes of future historians is proceeding apace. It is also proceeding futilely. The man was too big; too raw; too powerful to lend credence to the gentlemanly populist that is being depicted in the Austin mausoleum where people who barely knew him are constructing a shrine. The genie will not stay in the bottle! He was magnificent but he was also crude, petty, surprisingly naive along certain lines, and ridden by nameless terrors. The magnificence is entitled to full attention but it will not separate itself from the darker side of his nature.

In this book, I am not quoting Lyndon Johnson's thoughts but interpreting them. We began growing apart almost as soon as he entered the White House, but we were quite close during the Senate days. I am not altogether certain how much of the thinking was really his and how much was my interpretation of his thinking. He had a habit of adopting all useful thoughts as his own, and often the originator of highly important ideas would forget his or her own authorship in a matter of hours and be ready to swear that the whole thing originated in the brain of "the Leader."

My original mistake was to assume that I could write this book without putting myself into it. This was partly an ingrained habit from the Johnson days and partly an effort to be "fair" and objective. I should have known better. Kierkegaard defines objectivity as the concept of thinking without a thinker, and Ortega y Gasset says that the greatest of all delusions is that human beings have the capacity to see the world as it would be if they were not there to look at it. I have dropped the delusions.

At any rate, here it is and I wish I had written it many years ago. The effort of writing has cleared up my own views to me. I hope it will be helpful to others. I do not expect this to be either the last or the definitive word on Lyndon B. Johnson. There will be many years before either work is written. He was simply too big to be put on paper so close to his death. This, however, is my contribution to an understanding of a man who played an extraordinary role in our history and whose deeds will remain with us — for both good and evil — for many, many decades.

1

The Potemkin Village

The ice that blocked the Dnieper River thawed early in 1787 and by May a highly unusual flotilla began a journey downstream from Kiev. In the lead was a grand vessel painted in dazzling colors and bearing all the symbols of royalty. On its deck, ensconced on a throne, sat one of the world's mightiest autocrats — Catherine the Great of Russia. At a respectful distance to the rear was an ostentatiously less ostentatious barge whose principal passenger crossed frequently to the more resplendent ship. He was Grigori Aleksandrovich Potemkin, known among his contemporaries as one of the world's craftiest manipulators of autocrats.

It was a pleasant journey which probably filled the czarina with roseate pictures of herself as Lady Bountiful. Happy, well-dressed peasants gathered in clusters to wave and dance in joy on the banks as she went past. The villages were clean and soundly built and obviously there was plenty of food left over from the previous harvest as the farmers made preparations for the spring planting. It was a scene of prosperity and national happiness well calculated to strengthen the confidence of Catherine in her chief adviser, who did such an excellent job in relieving her of what she considered the petty details of running the country.

1

Her viewpoint might have changed somewhat had she known that the peasants had been drilled — and, to some extent, clothed — by Potemkin agents and that the villages had been refurbished by his orders. Some of them were little more than what today would be motion picture "flats" set up for the camera lens only. These were to become known in history as "Potemkin villages," structures which had no purpose other than to present a façade of strength and order.

This episode always comes to my mind when I think of Lyndon Baines Johnson. Of course there are differences — in time, place, climate, language, and availability of water. But only one of the changes is really important. It is that throughout his life, Johnson played the role of both Catherine and Potemkin. He constructed his own villages and then looked upon them and declared them good. Whatever was unsatisfactory in his life he recast into the mold he desired and then convinced himself (and an astonishingly great number of people) that the recasting was the reality and the original had never existed.

To make the analogy valid, it must be realized that both Catherine and Potemkin were people of power who successfully manipulated the real strengths of Russia behind the façade on the banks of the Dnieper and who altered the course of world history. Similarly with Lyndon B. Johnson. I do not know, for example, whether he began with a deep conviction of the moral rightness of the civil rights cause or whether his dedication arose from expediency. In either case, he profoundly changed national policy on the treatment of minorities and I believe that he acted out of pure motives regardless of their origin. He had a remarkable capacity to convince himself that he held the principles he should hold at any given time, and there was something charming about the air of injured innocence with which he would treat anyone who brought forth evidence that he had held other views in the past. It was not an act. His whole life was lived in the present and he was tenacious in his conviction that history always conformed to current necessities. He even carried this rule into the field of autobiography, where elementary — and sometimes important — facts about his past became completely lost as he told and retold them.

Let it again be clear that this book is not intended as a biography. I have a great deal of pity for anyone who undertakes the task. Nothing can be more confusing than to straighten out the conflicting stories of his childhood and his youth. His own accounts were at sharp variance with those of his contemporaries in Johnson City, San Marcos, and Austin, Texas, but the differences do not emerge without deep probing. The strength of his personality was so great that people who knew the truth found themselves subconsciously seeing the past the way he saw it. Frequently, in searching for the reality of some incident out of his college years, I sensed my problem was to awaken those whom I was interviewing from an hypnotic trance.

To complicate the picture, his *own* view of what had happened frequently shifted. To the outside world, this appeared as a form of mendacity. It is my firm belief, from close association over a number of years, that the man never told a deliberate lie. But he had a fantastic capacity to persuade himself that the "truth" which was convenient for the present was *the truth* and anything that conflicted with it was the prevarication of enemies. He literally willed what was in his mind to be reality and, as he was a master at imposing his will upon the people, the society, and the world around him, he saw no reason for history to be exempt from the process.

At times, this trait could place him into ludicrous postures. I have a vivid recollection of his "good will" visit to Cyprus as vice president one year after the island had been granted its independence. The animosity between the Greek majority and the Turkish minority was so high that it was difficult to keep one's face straight in describing the place as a nation. Our visit was the first occasion for unveiling the Cypriot flag but there was still no agreement on a national anthem, and the formal exchange of courtesies at the airport consisted of a band playing "The Star Spangled Banner" for the United States and then responding with a series of British bugle calls.

A by-product of the conflict was intense Greek dislike — and intense Turkish good will — for the United States. Both sentiments were based on the realization that the American fleet in the Mediterranean was the only force preventing the Greek majority from driving the Turkish minority into the sea. Both sides made their viewpoint clear when Lyndon B. Johnson toured Nicosia, the capital city, on the second day of his visit.

Our first stop was Ataturk Square, where Johnson received one of the most tumultuous demonstrations of his lifetime. Practically every Turk in the area had turned out — singing, dancing, shouting, cheering. Pushing the cavalcade through the crowds could be done only with the greatest of difficulty — particularly as the vice president insisted on leaving his automobile to shake hands with the demonstrators. At that point, he was a very happy politician.

Venizelos Square — the center of the Greek area — was a different scene altogether. It was saved from being totally empty only by a teen-age boy and a teen-age girl sitting (quite close to each other) on a park bench in total oblivion of the vice president of the United States or even of Cyprus. Hannibal, trooping through with a herd of elephants, would not have distracted them.

A swing through the Greek residential sections beyond the square produced very little more. People walking the streets were obviously attending to business, and their reaction to the cavalcade ranged from mild surprise that it was there at all to bitter distaste on the faces of those who recognized the American flags. The American reporters who were with us were traveling with me in an automobile driven by an English-speaking Turkish chauffeur who was careful to call everyone's attention to the contrast between the two receptions.

The American newsmen wrote the obvious accounts — a warm welcome from the Turks and a boycott from the Greeks. These stories were not intended to derogate Johnson. Obviously, the Cypriot reactions were based upon the posture of the United States of which Johnson was merely a symbol. There was nothing personal and none of his countrymen could have expected anything different.

The next morning, I was called into Johnson's suite in the Nicosia Hotel. The American newspapers, flown to him daily, had arrived already and he was in a towering rage. I was ordered to summon the journalists for a confrontation.

"That God-damned press has lied about me enough," he bellowed. "They have been trying to 'get me' ever since we started this trip. I am not going to let them do to me what they did to Dick Nixon."

I had not seen the papers, as they had gone directly to him before he got out of bed. I probed to get at the cause of his fury — no simple feat as he was almost incoherent. Finally, the facts emerged. He was *convinced* that the stories about the Greek boycott had been written only to portray him to the American public as unpopular with people in other countries. He thought that the reporters traveling with us were allies of Robert Kennedy, whom he suspected of having engineered the news stories of the hostile crowds who greeted Richard M. Nixon when he visited Venezuela as vice president. He pointed out that on our way in from the airport we had passed through a rural Greek village where there had been cheers from men and women dancing in the streets. This, he insisted, should have been proof enough to the press that "I am just as popular with the Greeks as I am with the Turks."

Somehow, I talked him out of his "showdown" with the press — a process that could have resulted in nothing but stories questioning his sanity. But the incident stuck in my mind, not just because it was so strange but because it shed insight into Johnson's psychology and his view of the world in which he lived. His reactions were merely a logical response to his interpretation of the social universe around him.

To place what happened in perspective, it is necessary to understand that he regarded the political process *entirely* in terms of popularity. His mind, shaped in the intensely personal arena of Texas politics, rejected the concept that friendly or hostile receptions to visiting dignitaries could be dictated by attitudes toward the nation they represented. Thus, the crowds in Venezuela who jeered and attempted to spit at Nixon were expressing hatred of Nixon as a man, rather than Nixon as a symbol of the United States. Similarly, if the press said that he had received a cold reception from the Greeks, it was saying that the Greeks hated him *as Lyndon B. Johnson*, rather than as a symbol of American foreign policy which they found objectionable.

The next step in his mental process was a conviction that facts should be properly arranged — at all times — to serve a purpose. His purpose — to demonstrate that he was popular with the people in the countries that he visited — was best served by putting together the reception in the Greek village with the reception in the Turkish quarter of Nicosia. The press had put a different set of facts together and therefore it was obvious to him that they were serving the purposes of another man. That other man had to be Robert Kennedy, whom he regarded as the focal point for all of the forces who sought the downfall of Lyndon B. Johnson.

As a corollary, it should be noted that he regarded journalists as critics rather than as purveyors of information. He could not believe that any story about a political personality had been written just because something had happened. In his mind, it was something that had been inspired by either the friends or the foes of the personality. It was also something that passed judgment, pro or con, upon the popularity and the performance of political leaders in general.

Much more will, of necessity, be devoted to Johnson's relationships with the press in a later chapter. For an overview, however, it is sufficient to make the point that he regarded the press as a battlefield for competing politicians rather than an essential part of the political and governing process. Therefore, he engaged in a relentless search for press agents who could divert the press into writing harmless stories while he proceeded with the serious business of government.

It is at this point that we come to a major key to the Johnson political profile. He *was* an intensely serious man with intensely serious purposes. But he did not believe those purposes could be accomplished through public discussion. He was absolutely convinced that achievement was possible only through careful negotiation in quiet backrooms where public passions could not intrude. Open debate did serve some purposes, of course. It gave the leaders time to work out details before bringing issues to a vote and, properly managed, it produced a record that might be useful in the future. But under no circumstances was it to be allowed to interfere with the negotiations that were really producing a solution.

There is much to be said for his approach. His triumphant progress as Senate Democratic leader did depend upon his capacity to use the Senate floor as a diversionary device, which enabled him to stay out of the spotlight while horse-trading with the chieftains of different factions. It is doubtful whether any other tactics would have succeeded in reunifying the Senate Democrats after the 1952 defeat or in producing enactment of the Civil Rights Act of 1957.

Unfortunately, he elevated what was only a tactic, which might be justified under some circumstances, to a principle useful at any and all times. He abhorred dissent to a point where he sought to quell it long before protagonists had talked themselves out. It was one thing to maneuver people into a form of unity over an issue such as civil rights where everyone on either side was already talked out but did not know how to stop. It was another thing to close debate on American participation in the Vietnamese war, where virtually nothing had been said in advance and entry had come about through a process of mindless drifting. (It should be added that he succeeded in closing the debate only in the White House and could not understand just why it persisted in the nation as a whole.)

It should be stressed — to his credit — that he never expressed a desire to suppress dissent by force. He was not a dictator and did not seek dictatorial powers. At any moment — even when his White House setbacks produced a touch of paranoia — he was willing to give serious consideration to opposing points of view. However, he wanted those points of view to be brought to him by men he regarded as "responsible" leaders representing substantial numbers of people and willing to negotiate against other leaders to obtain the best possible "deal" for their constituencies. He could not see the purpose of public debate, which he regarded at best as unnecessary and always as inflammatory and disruptive of progress.

A democracy will always produce parliaments with a strong leavening of such men and women — pragmatic, achievement oriented, impatient with ideological hair splitting. It is doubtful whether democratic systems could work without such leaders. Debate never reaches complete agreement, and somewhere along the line it is essential to put a temporary halt to divisive words and find means of getting something done. This step will inevitably result in log-rolling, a pejorative phrase we apply to the give-and-take process of democracy. It may help in understanding the government of the United States to substitute another, and more descriptive, phrase — accommodation of divergent points of view.

In accommodating different points of view, Johnson was a superb craftsman. He did *not*, however, understand democratic government as a two-step process in which negotiation was only one phase. The role of public debate in securing popular assent to policies and, ultimately, national unity was a concept he could not grasp. Talk, to him, had true meaning only when it was directed to the problem of how to get something done. Discussions of goals and ethics were merely exercises in posturing, and he had no patience with such goings-on.

An important element in his success as Democratic leader of the Senate was the historical timing of his ascendancy to power. He assumed the floor manager's post at a period when a number of basic issues had been talked to death without any real resolution. In addition to civil rights, they included such matters as health care, adequate housing for all Americans, farm subsidies, Social Security extension to virtually the entire population, and, most basic of all, the question of whether the federal government should intervene *whenever* citizens were in trouble. In every instance, debate had become repetitive. It continued only because antagonists had become victims of habit, incapable of sitting down with each other and finding sensible solutions.

For a man of Johnson's talents, the timing could not have been better. His genuine political principles were simple and in step with the national mood. At heart, he was a New Deal populist who believed that all problems could be solved by putting floors under wages and farm prices; guaranteeing cheap electric power to all citizens; enacting a system of universal health care; and granting all young people a free education up through graduate work in a university. As far as he was concerned, these were all goals which could not be questioned. The only subject for discussion was how the most could be made out of them at any given time. He later added to his list the attainment of civil rights for blacks — not, in my judgment, solely because he had presidential aspirations but simply because he convinced himself that the status of black minorities was similar to the life he had led as a very poor boy in Johnson City, Texas.

His was not an unprincipled political philosophy even though it was simplistic. But it was one which freed him from allegiances that had precluded accomplishment by earlier Democratic (or Republican) leaders. He thought of the Senate as a workshop for resolving political, social, and economic problems rather than as an arena of conflict for contrasting ideologies. Therefore, he did not label senators as Democratic and Republican or liberal and conservative but as "work horses" and "show horses" (both pet phrases). He was equally at home with the conservative Republican Everett M. Dirksen and the liberal Democrat John O. Pastore — because both were "work horses." He was similarly uncomfortable with the liberal Republican Jake Javits and the conservative Democrat Frank Lausche, because both were "show horses." A leader such as LBJ, who was capable of crossing both party and ideological lines to organize the "work horses," was bound, ultimately, to take over the Senate. He had grasped the chess principle of capturing the center row, even though he may never have heard of chess.

Once the "center" was firmly in hand, debate became not only boring but irrelevant. Liberals were cautioned successfully not to discuss what they regarded as the inadequacies of Johnson legislation because such discussion threatened to divide moderate ranks and kill liberal legislation. Conservatives were muted because they were taught to fear the risk of driving moderates into the liberal camp and thus bringing down on their heads even more "radical" legislation. It was a position of tremendous strength as long as the man in the center knew what he wanted.

It was not so strong, however, when he was confronted with issues that did not fit the classic New Deal, populist pattern. These began to arise during the Korean War, which, however justified America's intervention may have been, could not truthfully be presented as a straightforward defense of American soil against a potential aggressor. The Asian conflict spawned a series of subsidiary issues — the military draft; control of private productive facilities to insure adequate supplies for the armed forces; management of the nation's economy to avoid inflation. These problems were relatively manageable during the fighting in Korea, where it was at least possible to establish lines and claim a "victory" by pushing "the enemy" back behind them. But in Vietnam, where there was no possibility of locating a geographical "victory" point, they got completely out of hand. In the end, they brought about his downfall because the public could not see any reward for the sacrifice.

The unhappy ending of the Johnson political story, however, cannot detract from the man's fascination. He was a tremendous figure — a combination of complexities and simplicities that bewildered all observers. He could be extremely shrewd in dealing with political contemporaries and astoundingly gullible in the selection of his personal advisers. He was capable of taking tremendous risks in some directions and of exhibiting extraordinary timidity in others. He had a deep and compassionate understanding of the economic underdog but no comprehension of the feelings of those who felt they had been displaced by the machinations of mass society. The fact that a generation of Americans could be alienated from the values of their forefathers was something beyond his ken.

It is doubtful whether the political triumphs of his Senate and early presidential periods could be repeated today. It is a different world — partly because he himself made it so. The people with whom he dealt so successfully are gone, to be replaced by others who do not react to the levers he manipulated so well. The polity has set new goals which would seem very strange indeed to a Texas boy born into relative poverty in the early part of the century, when the burning American dream was to move upward economically.

Regardless of how things have changed, however, Lyndon Baines Johnson was *the* consummate political leader of his era. Despite his weaknesses, he had a profound understanding of the workings of America's governmental system. For this alone, he is worth careful scrutiny. The present can be understood only in terms of the past, and there is an important slice of our past in which he was the principal moving force. He acted and the nation reacted. How future

history will treat his presidency is anyone's guess. I do not pretend to
know and I am not going to make a stab at it. He will obviously occupy
many pages but whether they will be laudatory or condemnatory is
for the future to reveal. Of one thing, however, I am confident. No
one will ever be able to look at him without concluding that he was
either the most, or one of the most, fascinating of the presidential
personalities of the twentieth century.

2

A Word Is a Word Is a Word

Preaching in All Saints Cathedral on the morning this was written, Father Leech gave me the focal point for this chapter. His sermon was directed at sham piety, which he characterized as a mythical book entitled: *Humility and How I Achieved It*. "Lyndon Johnson wrote that," I murmured in a spontaneous reaction. A glare from the occupant of a neighboring pew made it clear that my voice level was enough to carry quite a few feet. I bowed my head to cover my confusion while hoping that others would take my gesture as a pious apology. To myself, however, I said: "But it's true. If there is such a book, *he* wrote it."

Actually, it was only partially true. Lyndon B. Johnson would never have written that — or any other — book. But had the suggestion been made to him, he would have turned it over to a speech writer. Furthermore, once it had been completed — and revised by four or five of his friends — he would have issued the volume under his own name in full confidence that it would provide adequate evidence of his essential modesty. Within a week, people on four or five mailing lists would have received autographed copies with an accompanying note: "I thought you would like to know about my most lovable characteristic, which is humility."

Many people, of course, might do something like this (naturally with variations) to con the public. What makes LBJ unique is that he would not only have presented the book as evidence of humility but would have believed that it proved the point. He would never have grasped the irony in either the title or the note. He was the ideal target for the Irish bull. In his mind, the printed word conferred qualities of grace upon those to whom it referred. His conviction on this question bordered on superstition. He subscribed to what was essentially a primitive form of word magic and he cared very much about the words of characterization.

Unfortunately, he did not hold in any awe the words that were designed to stir or unite the public for action. As far as he was concerned, a speech was a performance whose success was measured by the immediate reaction of the audience. He could not see it as a force permitting or limiting future moves and he regarded it as very unfair for anyone to cite past addresses as contrary to present intentions. Meditating upon this trait, Hugh Sidey — Time-Life presidential "expert" — once said that "he has no respect for the integrity of the language."

Like mine, Sidey's remark was only partially true. He *did* have respect for the integrity of the words involved in a "deal" and when he was engaged in negotiations, his language was terse and to the point. He could not fairly be accused of going back on his word once he had given it. The difficulty was his inability to see a public speech as anything other than a crowd pleaser. Part of this was a result of the Victorian-type declamation he had been taught by his mother. More important, however, was his inability to trace a connection between public words and action. His concept of oratory was that of a device to produce moods. That it could also educate and unify people behind a program was a thought that he regarded as highly esoteric.

Of course, he presented programs. In 1955, following his first heart attack, he presented an eleven-point program for the Democratic Party that catapulted him back into a leadership position which others had thought he would have to forgo because of his physical condition. As president, he fired programs at Congress with a bewildering rapidity and succeeded in securing passage of most of them. But the programs were fed to him by others and he paid little attention to how they were carried out. Somehow, he assumed that they would be self-operating.

Furthermore, it did not bother him to abandon a program once he concluded that it had lost its public appeal. A prime example was the exploration of outer space, sparked by the successful Soviet launch of two satellites in the fall of 1957. He seized the opportunity to launch a brilliantly conducted series of hearings not only upon the level of America's outer space technology but also upon its defense posture. This may well have been the most important of all steps in his march to the presidency because it identified him in the public mind with an issue that transcended ordinary political horse trading. It also helped that the Eisenhower administration saw fit to pooh-pooh the whole issue — thus casting Lyndon B. Johnson in the role of a man of vision opposed by routine political hacks who could not see the shape of the future.

Unfortunately, Johnson himself could see the issue only in terms of newspaper space and public attention. It did not involve poverty, education, or economic opportunity — problems which really held his attention. Therefore, as column inches devoted to outer space dwindled and as polls registered a diminution of popular interest, he virtually abandoned the entire project. Worried assistants, who realized that his language had been too strong to close the books with nothing accomplished, pushed him into sponsoring and securing the passage of the outer space act, which established NASA and ultimately led to the landing on the moon. But this feat was accomplished only by shoving papers into his hand to be read on the floor of the Senate. He made it clear that he was going through the motions only to quiet the insistent demands of his staff. In later years, when he was reaping the public-image benefits of NASA achievements, he persuaded himself that they had taken place because of *his* prodding of *his* colleagues and *his* staff.

Johnson's inability to connect words with reality also produced nightmares for his speech writers. His only instructions were "Do me a speech," which really meant "Give me a script so I can entertain the audience." What he wanted was a fundamentalist sermon of the "Come to Jesus" variety without being too specific on the pathway to salvation. Invariably, he asked for a "proposal" to be placed in the speech. But it was clear that the proposal should be noncontroversial and acceptable to all hearers. Occasionally, this situation actually produced some accomplishment — such as the time that a desperate speech writer embellished a talk by suggesting the establishment of an "East-West" educational center on Hawaii where scholars from both hemispheres could be brought together for mutual understanding. The delegate from Hawaii — Jack Burns — was an astute operator who seized upon the address as a springboard for establishing the center. It worked.

Perhaps the outstanding example of his attitude took place during his good-will tour to Asia when he was vice president. He and Ayub Khan, the president of Pakistan, became warm friends on the spot. As a result, Johnson decided to make his visit truly memorable by producing something other than the dreary communiques put together by State Department officials when there really is not very much to say after an international meeting. A secretary was hastily summoned and he started to dictate:

"The vice president of the United States and the president of Pakistan agree that government is legitimate only when it is based upon the will of the governed. . . ."

"My God," gasped an assistant. "This country has been under martial law for the past five years." He was finally persuaded that it would not be politic to present Ayub Khan with what appeared to be a criticism of the Pakistani form of government. But it was clear that he was only half-convinced. He could not see anything wrong with the use of noble words.

He did, however, as stated earlier, understand the meaning of words when he was confronted with what he regarded as reality. He was impatient with verbosity or ornate adjectives when they were included in an "action memo." And when he was engaged in negotiations over a real issue, his language was always to the point — direct, meaningful, and memorable. He could get action and he could get it fast. In legislative floor-strategy sessions, he could cut off anyone who started to discuss the merits of a bill with a curt: "We know that! What we want to know is where we get the votes."

Actually, he usually did *not* "know that." His only substantive ideology was, as he would put it, to "be for the people — spelled pee-pul" — and he looked upon anything beyond that as window dressing. During the 1950s, it was impossible to win statewide office in Texas without at least dividing the conservative vote. He saw nothing unethical about employing conservative language in his home state while using his Senate position to further the cause of medical care, public power, Social Security, and, ultimately, civil rights for the black minorities. The result was liberal distrust for his rhetoric and conservative distrust for his actions. Nevertheless, in terms of Texas politics, the tactic worked. Neither conservatives nor liberals dared to desert him completely out of fear that it might lead to a triumph for the other side.

This distrust did nothing to impair his effectiveness in the Senate, where, despite the popular impression, language has little to do with the passage of legislation. The Senate is the world's purest political body — an institution whose function is to measure the political forces behind issues and determine the resolution that is the most likely to be acceptable to all parties concerned — or, at least, to all substantial parties concerned. When a bill reaches the floor — or when it becomes apparent that a bill will reach the floor — a probing process begins to find out which senatorial commitments are irrevocable, which can be modified, and which can be forgotten completely. The primary function of debate is to gain time. An occasional speech sways votes but this is rare — very rare.

The influential members of the Senate did not care in the slightest that Johnson was making public speeches which had little or no relationship to his voting record. What impressed them was his ability to find compromise points that put together majorities to enact legislation. Frequently, the compromises offered one party nothing but a face-saver (the 1957 Civil Rights Bill, for example, gave the Southern senators only a mythical claim that they had preserved jury trial rights for their constituents). But this was still better than humiliation. Consequently, there was never a moment during his eight years of leadership that his position faced a truly serious challenge. Many senators disliked him intensely but they were unwilling to take a chance on a different type of floor management.

When he reached the presidency, however, Johnson's cavalier attitude toward public speech took on a different aspect. To be successful, a president must have an ability to maneuver politically. But that is only a part — and not the most important part — of his job. Fundamentally, the president is there to lead the nation — to shape attitudes, to inspire public effort, to preserve national unity. He can, of course, make meaningless "Christ, how the wind blew" speeches and if he does not deliver them too often, he will be forgiven. But when his words have meaning in the dictionary sense, the American people take them seriously and expect him to stand by them. They can no longer be regarded solely as stimuli to a mood.

The Johnson weakness did not become immediately apparent on his assumption of the presidency. During his first few months in office, the only speech-making necessary consisted of appeals for national unity and to carry on the programs advanced by the martyred John F. Kennedy. Plenty of Kennedy speech writers were available to produce this kind of rhetoric and they were happy to do so. They were using the LBJ voice to glorify the man to whom their hearts truly belonged.

Even more important, however, Congress had enacted very little important legislation during the Kennedy regime and had quite a backlog of unfinished legislative business. Johnson applied himself with gusto to cleaning up that backlog — a task he understood thoroughly. In effect, the majority leader's office had been moved from the third floor of the Capitol to the first floor of the White House and every legislative triumph added further luster to the LBJ halo.

During this period, the Johnson performance was magnificent. Whatever else history may say about him, it should grant the highest marks to his reassurance of a nation that had been badly shaken by the first presidential assassination in decades. He understood the problem and responded by consciously demonstrating the enduring strength of America's institutions.

His difficulties really began in the 1964 campaign. It is doubtful whether any other man in American history piled up so many troubles for himself in conducting a successful drive for elective office. The irony of the whole thing was that it was totally unnecessary. He could have kept his mouth shut and won without making an effort — perhaps not by the same margin but still decisively.

Barry Goldwater, the Republican candidate, was of the breed of politicians who are much more interested in converts than in votes. He had the same interest in ideological purity that old-time revivalist preachers had in adherence to the word and the letter of the Bible. In effect, Goldwater did not want anyone to come to him who had not been "washed in the blood of the Lamb." A cardinal tenet of his ideological purism was that the United States should be strong in a military sense — stronger than any other nation in the world.

For those who know Barry Goldwater, the split between his personality and his ideology is a source of perpetual wonderment. He is a decent, honorable, gentle, kindly person whose major hobby is collecting Navajo dolls but whose speeches are shot through with fire, brimstone, and right-wing revolutionary rhetoric. Nothing is more incongruous than hearing this lovable, avuncular man call for lobbing an ICBM "down into the gent's room in the Kremlin."

It became obvious right from the start that the most effective campaign speeches for Lyndon Johnson were being made by Barry Goldwater himself. He selected the Tennessee Valley as the site for a speech calling for the sale of TVA. He selected Florida as the area where he would call for a downward revision of Social Security. And everywhere he went, he rattled atomic sabers — bellicose speeches that left the impression that the United States, should he win the presidency, would be at war the day after his inauguration.

Why Lyndon Johnson decided to campaign at all was something I could never fathom. I think it was entirely a reaction to boredom. All he really had to do was to stay in Washington and tend to the presidency — with an occasional release of information on classified weapons systems to demonstrate that the military posture of the United States was sound. But campaign he did and, as always in the past, he was carried away by his own rhetoric. He set out to prove what the voters already believed — that he was a sensible man who would keep the United States both strong and out of war.

At every stop along the airplane trail, he hammered away at the peace theme. He would never "send American boys to do the fighting that should be done by Asian boys." He was ready to help America's allies who were fighting communism but not by sending troops — only by sending supplies and munitions. The task of a president was to build a "Great Society" — not to destroy it in an atomic war where "big ones" would be lobbed into toilets.

There is no doubt that he meant every word of it — as he always meant every word. Neither is there any doubt that it was unnecessary. Goldwater was making every point much more vividly and could be trusted to continue doing so. The only result of the LBJ campaign was to produce a record that would haunt him as the casualty lists piled in from Vietnam. His last years in the White House were spent in an effort to prove that he had not said those things or at least had not said them in the context presented by the press. It was futile. It is probable that Vietnam, under any circumstances, would have led to a verdict of bad judgment — perhaps, even monstrously bad judgment. But the campaign of 1964 also opened him to a charge of duplicity which will certainly becloud the historical record.

Lyndon B. Johnson did not regard himself as guilty of duplicity and I tend to agree with him even though he said one thing and did another. In my judgment he was a victim of his inability to connect public words with public action — not an uncommon failing of politicians. The forces that propelled him into Vietnam were complex and shall be dealt with in a later chapter. But when examined closely, the mistakes were all of bad judgment rather than deliberate misdirection.

It may well be that in the final analysis, Lyndon Johnson's failure to understand the role of the communication process in a democratic society contributed more than anything else to his undoing. He could not understand the distinction between a speech and a soliloquy in a play. To him, both were intended to move the audience — but only to wild applause. He did not even understand the question of using words that were appropriate. He once demanded from his staff several paragraphs of humor to go into a Rose Garden statement on behalf of efforts to improve the lot of retarded children.

He could be hypnotized by his own rhetoric. And on occasion, when he had something to say that would arouse an audience, he would throw discretion to the winds and produce outrageous statements which took months of patient work to correct. While still a senator, he flew to a town in East Texas equipped with a speech mildly critical of the United Nations. It had been prepared on the realization that the UN was highly unpopular in East Texas and he had to exhibit at least a semblance of independence from the "internationalists." The critical words were meaningless and cancelled themselves out. But his blood began to surge as he recognized the popularity they would have with the audience. By the time he reached the dining hall, every qualifying word had been eliminated and, to the horror of his staff in Austin, stories appeared the next day in which he was quoted as virtually ordering the United Nations to get out of the United States. It was not a very comfortable platform for the Democratic leader of the United States Senate but after several weeks of maneuvering, he managed to get it lost.

In this instance forces were at hand to bring him back to reality. His Democratic colleagues in the Senate — as well as his staff — minced no words in telling him bluntly that he had made a major boner. What was intriguing, however, was his bewilderment when he discovered his mistake. To him, a speech was a speech and it had not occurred to him that he might have to live with the words. In the White House, neither his staff nor his colleagues could speak to him in the "mother tongue." Perhaps this had something to do with Vietnam. He did not realize in his own mind that his words were misleading and eventually he became their prisoner.

In saying this, I am not trying to find an excuse for the fact that whatever he intended, the result in Vietnam was to mislead the public. Although I am convinced he did not mean to do so, the public *was* misled, and with this his soul must live through all eternity. I am not attempting here, however, to pass judgment on LBJ. I am trying to contribute some insights that might help the understanding of this man. Vietnam is not the first example in history of a hell whose access roads were paved with good intentions and I doubt whether it will be the last.

3

The Po' Boy Triumphant

All questions about the personality of Lyndon B. Johnson are difficult to answer. The man was an enigma even to himself. At times he obviously was at a loss to determine his own identity. He had the actor's knack for assuming any character required by the current plot and, like many theatrical people I have known, was not quite certain of the role he should be playing when there was no audience.

He was a gifted mimic who could easily have made his living on the vaudeville stage. His caricatures of people he did not like — Bobby Kennedy, Adlai Stevenson, Estes Kefauver, Richard Nixon, for example — were cruel but irresistibly comic. He had no other form of humor — except for the practical joke — and whatever wit was found in his speeches invariably came from a ghost. The problem with his mimicry was that he extended it beyond all bounds. He had an idea that he could become a great man by imitating great men and this led to some odd moments.

Ghost writers were constantly receiving instructions to "write like Roosevelt" or "write like Churchill" — two styles which sat awkwardly on his shoulders. He once lectured his staff on food habits, insisting that they stick to salads containing only three shrimp because that was what he had seen on the luncheon table of Secretary of

Defense Robert S. McNamara, a man he at one time admired greatly. An article describing President John F. Kennedy as an obsessive soup eater led to the purchase of crates of canned soup to be taken on every trip. Actually Johnson was not very fond of the stuff but one of the companies put out a chili-bean product he could swallow.

The problem of finding the real Lyndon B. Johnson was further complicated by the advent of television film and tape. This gave him an opportunity to study his public appearances and, Pygmalion-like, seek to change his image. This meant a series of hair stylings; continual changes in the cut of his clothes; and interminable arguments over the merits of horned rim versus rimless glasses. For a while, he tried contact lenses but the shape of his eyeballs was wrong. He could not stand the agony — particularly under the glare of television and newsreel lights.

Nevertheless, a real Lyndon B. Johnson could be found not by listening to his words but by watching what he did. There were political issues upon which he never deviated and in these are the clues to what was genuine about his personality. At bottom it was a burning desire to make life easier for those who had to struggle up from the bottom. His interpretation of what was required might be open to question but not his desire to act.

The point emerges with sharp clarity in an examination of his views on education. Nothing was in his thoughts more often. He sought guarantees that every boy or girl in the United States "could have all the education he or she can take." He was actually superstitious about the subject, and at times one expected him to advocate college as a cure for dandruff or university as a specific for sore throats.

At the heart of the matter was his conviction that education was the pathway out of poverty. He had no real interest in "academic subjects." The best he could say for philosophy was that it produced homilies to insert in his talks and he regarded historians as speech writers. What he sought was a "practical" education which would turn out income-earning, tax-paying citizens. This led him to equate a beauty school with a university and to speak of his cook, who had attended a training institute for black servants, as "that college-educated woman."

This situation brought about a seeming paradox. No man did more to provide higher education with funds for teaching students. No man was more detested by the academic community. The problem was that they were using the word "education" to describe different things. To them, the purpose of the exercise was to ground young people in the biological, physical, humanistic, and social disciplines. To him, the purpose was to open up opportunities for the oppressed and the underprivileged. The professors thought of the middle class; he thought of the cotton fields and the slums.

The Johnson predilection for the underdog had an unexpected result. It was a genuine interest in the problems of the Third World — that part of the globe which somehow missed out on the benefits of the industrial revolution. He read Barbara Ward's book *Rich Nations, Poor Nations* over and over again, and one of the factors behind his persistence in prosecuting the war in Vietnam was a poorly digested concept that the United States could raise the standard of living in that nation if only the Communists could be repulsed. On such issues he was very simplistic.

The fundamental Johnsonian view of the universe was that of the rural "po' boy" born to poverty and determined to exact vengeance from the aristrocrats he regarded as holding him in contempt. This attitude often produced results that were bewildering to many of his Northern colleagues whose political principles were almost identical to his but who had not felt the social sting of being an underdog in the hog and hominy belt. They could not comprehend his tolerance for Dixie demagogues who, in Northern minds, were contemptible charlatans. To him, they were the voice of the dispossessed of the earth. He especially admired Huey Long and defended him consistently as the man who brought Louisiana rednecks and Cajuns out of the muck and gave creole aristocrats the comeuppance they had earned by decades of arrogance.

The opposite side of the coin was that he stood in some awe of men who could lay some claim to the American version of "blue blood" — the Bundys, the Lodges, the Saltonstalls. This awe, however, led him to strike out savagely whenever he could at members of the Northeastern "establishment" or people who looked like them. Adlai Stevenson brought out his worst instincts. He would spend long periods at gatherings of those he regarded as "real men" regaling the audience with imitations of Stevenson's accent (his favorite was the pronunciation of "tomato" as "tomawto") and characteristics he regarded as effeminate. The high point came at a banquet of Democratic leaders where, as he later bragged, in making a speech, he graced former President Harry S. Truman with a low bow and succeeded, in the same motion, in pushing his posterior within an inch of Steven-

son's face. That story was told and retold to so many people so many
times in succeeding years that I can repeat it in my sleep. I do not
know whether this really happened but the story did not endear him
to me or to many other people.

As far as the middle class — Northern variety — was concerned, he
was completely bewildered unless they were members of a minority
group. He could relate both to Jewish workers and to Jewish
businessmen but he had troubles with other ethnic groups who had
"made it," such as the Irish. His problems in dealing with the "middle
class" became very apparent in his "good-will" travels as vice president. He did well in the Third World; poorly in more advanced
countries.

His appearance touched off massive and enthusiastic demonstrations among the illiterate and poverty-stricken hordes in Vietnam,
India, Pakistan, Iran, and Persia. Italian shipyard workers in Naples
put on one of the most exuberant demonstrations in the history of that
exuberant city. Latin peasants turned his visits into fiestas and
Lebanese construction crews cheered even to his satisfaction. He was
far less successful with the leaders of those nations, particularly
Nehru of India, and his triumphal procession through Naples was not
repeated in much more sophisticated Rome, where his only crowd
consisted of American Embassy employees ordered to station themselves at a street corner as he went by.

Probably many of the demonstrations were arranged by the gov-
ernments. But this is not a sufficient explanation. It was impossible to
walk through the crowds surrounding his cavalcades in Saigon, Agra,
Karachi, Teheran, or Ankara without realizing that he was striking
responsive chords. The people understood him and he understood
them. He knew what to say to members of cultures that were alien to
him in every respect but a common understanding of poverty and the
stigma of inferiority.

In a tiny village outside Agra, for example, he stopped alongside of
a well from which the Indian peasants drew water by hand in a bucket
at the end of a long rope. Johnson pulled up a bucketful and then
turned to the crowd with an impromptu speech. Through an in-
terpreter, he explained that when he was a small boy in Texas, his
family had been supplied with water out of a similar well. Graphi-
cally, he described the efforts it took to bring up enough for the family
washing. The whole thing sounded cornball to a city boy like me until
I realized that he had the crowd's rapt attention. Sometimes, he said,

the rope would slip and burn the palms of his hands. Several of the villagers grinned and rubbed their palms together. Sometimes, the well would run dry and he would have to ride a donkey ten miles to the next water source. More grins from the audience. Even in translation, they knew — and appreciated — what this man was saying.

The talk ended with a description of the organization of farmers and ranchers in his district to form a rural electric cooperative on money borrowed from the U.S. government. I doubt whether the intricacies of REA financing made much sense to the Indian peasants. But they got a message which may well have justified the whole trip. What they heard was that this powerful man understood the problems of poor people and was part of a government that did something about those problems.

In contrast, his travels through Scandinavia were a veritable disaster. There was simply no rapport between the punctilious, middle-class burghers of these countries and Lyndon B. Johnson. In Sweden, he left behind a trail of angered officials — offended by his cavalier approach to time schedules and ceremonies, which are virtually sacrosanct in that nation. In Finland, he shocked officials and Helsinki journalists by walking over the graves of the people who were massacred at Rovaniemi. In Norway, he interrupted the service at a state banquet — in that country the equivalent of urinating on the table — by a meaningless conference with an aide who was placed in a position that blocked the waitresses when they came in with food. In Denmark, he touched off a nationwide cause celebre by having some of the furniture removed from his hotel bedroom and replaced with a king-size bed. (The furniture had been designed by a famous Danish craftsman and the action was viewed as a deliberate affront to the nation by a man who had won for himself a reputation throughout the Northern nations as a boor. Fortunately, Danes have a sense of humor and the end result was a series of humorous cartoons which everybody appreciated but LBJ.) Only in Iceland did things go reasonably well and that was because the stay lasted only a few hours.

In truth, he was a boor throughout the Scandinavian trip. He picked a fight with the *New York Times* correspondent over a triviality that would have gone unnoticed under other circumstances. He was curt in his meetings with officials and overly effusive in dancing with their wives. He left honor guards at rigid attention because he walked by them without the inspection demanded by protocol. There was not a single event for which his aides and the officials of the embassies did not have to apologize.

Part of the problem could be attributed to a kidney stone that was plaguing him. But this explanation — accepted by me and his other assistants at the time — was far too simple. In retrospect, it seems obvious that the neatness and order of the Scandinavian world went against his grain. A man of his extraordinary sensitivity to other people could not have failed to realize that he was antagonizing the entire leadership of Northern Europe. One or two incidents — such as the rudeness at the Norwegian banquet — could have been accidental. But the "incidents" were an unbroken string. They were deliberate and could have arisen only from his envy of a society which, in his terms, "had it made." Sweden, Finland, Norway, Denmark, and Iceland were bastions of respectability — the kind of "respectability" which he thought looked down on dirt farmers and rednecks and kept them "in their place."

In dealing with people he regarded as the victims of discrimination, his sensitivities were highly developed. At one time, he invited Adolpho Lopez Mateos, the president of Mexico, to the ranch. In preparation, his staff drew up a folder containing information for the press, including a section on San Antonio. Johnson exploded: "Get those dead Mexicans out of that picture." We were completely baffled, but fortunately, he calmed down and explained to us with surprising gentleness that a picture of the Alamo was not a tactful thing for presentation to Mexican officials and journalists. I am still bemused that I, who had no particular feelings on the subject, could have missed the obvious point whereas he, a Texan steeped in the chauvinistic lore of that state, caught it immediately. He was right — just as he was right a year later in persuading the Senate Rules Committee to remove from the Capitol a painting depicting the capture of Chapultepec by the United States Marines.

This pattern — sympathy for the underdog, resentment of those who were secure — becomes even clearer when his staff relationships are examined. He had many aides of varying backgrounds and capabilities. He sought advice from what he regarded as the "best brains," ranging all the way from the aristocratic Dean Acheson to tough Irish congressmen from New York. But his genuine warmth was reserved for the "po' boys" who had battled social discrimination to crawl out of the lower depths. It helped especially if they were Southern. This predilection led him into one of the most troublesome episodes of his career — the Bobby Baker case.

Bobby came to Washington as a small-town teen-ager in knee britches to take over a job as Senate page. He looked very much like the other pages — alert, quick, prematurely possessed of "smarts" akin to street wisdom. Also, like the other page boys, he had big dreams. He wanted to make a million dollars and he wanted to become governor of his native South Carolina. Unlike the others, however, he had a driving ambition to succeed and it was of such fantastic intensity that it had to be seen at close quarters to be credited. He also had certain talents — an amazing capacity to gather information and use it to attract the attention of men of power. One of those men was Lyndon B. Johnson, who became Bobby's patron and swiftly advanced him from a position as a straw boss over the Senate pages to secretary to the Senate Majority.

Under previous secretaries, the position had amounted to little more than the keeping of routine administrative records for the Senate Democrats and the provision of a quiet office near the Senate chamber where senior senators could adjourn for a quiet drink. Occasionally, a secretary would serve as a form of liaison between the Senate leadership and the press. But generally speaking, it was a sinecure. Bobby Baker changed all that. Suddenly, the Office of the Secretary to the Majority became the place to go for small favors. Even senators of power found it advisable to have a quiet conference with the secretary when they were seeking an extra patronage job or passage of relatively inconsequential bills. He could get things done.

Unfortunately for Bobby, he did not realize that his Senate "power" depended almost entirely upon the patronage of the Democratic Leader and that it was patronage that could be taken away as well as granted. He began to strike out on his own — a questionable stock deal involving a savings and loan company; some hanky-panky with a food machine vending corporation; a resort hotel on the Maryland coast financed by mysterious sources. With it all went a style of life that can be summed up in two words — booze and women. In both fields, Bobby was insatiable.

The Johnson staff became frantic. Bobby was obviously trouble — obviously to everyone except Lyndon B. Johnson. In LBJ's eyes, Bobby could do no wrong. When an assistant told him that Bobby was spreading the word that Johnson himself was "behind" the Maryland hotel (a story with no foundation whatsoever) the assistant narrowly escaped being fired. When another assistant questioned the propriety of establishing a Baker law office in Washington (while Bobby was still a Senate official) he was told curtly that LBJ did not appreciate the "snobbery" that was being expressed against a "poor Southern boy off the farm." Somehow, LBJ saw him as a symbol of himself — an outcast who had risen to prominence against the machinations of "respectable" society.

Despite the resemblances, Bobby Baker was not LBJ. The two men matched each other in background, ambition, and willingness to work. But at heart, Bobby was small time — a man who looked big for a brief period only because he had the patronage of a big man. He finally overreached himself — after Johnson had left the Senate — and Johnson spent a considerable portion of his vice presidential and presidential years trying to dissociate himself from his former protege. (To the hoots of the press corps, the members of the Senate, and virtually all of political Washington, he tried to claim that he had not participated in Bobby's advancement and, indeed, hardly knew his erstwhile protege.) Bobby went to jail and emerged with little left other than a connection with the Maryland hotel.

During the entire period, the Washington press corps combed records thoroughly seeking an improper connection between Johnson and Bobby Baker's shenanigans. It was never found, simply because it did not exist. The press corps, however, missed the point. What was important was the LBJ fondness for Bobby Baker — a fondness that amounted to doting. A study of Bobby Baker is an important key to a study of the LBJ personality. At bottom, what was happening was a sense of a connection with another soul who had spent his life sitting below the salt and who had shoved his way up to the more favored end of the table — shoved rudely, perhaps, but still effectively.

Bobby was not the end of his problem with ambitious Southern boys. As president, he made many staff appointments that were bewildering to those who had known him for years. The problem was that they had to be *ambitious* as well as Southern. Some of his people of impeccable Dixie heritage found themselves in the cold, not because they lacked ability but because they lacked sufficient chutzpah. As I puzzled over this phenomenon, one of my aunts, who died a few years ago, comes to mind. She was convinced that when she needed legal advice, it was best to get it from a "crooked lawyer." She thought he would cheat *for* her. Similarly, LBJ may well have believed that a young boy with burning ambitions would direct them in favor of his employer. Both he and my aunt learned much too late

that cheats and people who are "on the make" cheat only for themselves and work only to advance their own fortunes.

In exploring the LBJ personality it is well to begin with the Texas
boy who had within him a touch of the jacquerie and who saw the
world in terms of a battle between the comfortable and the dispossessed.

4

Political Sexpots

The association of sex and politics is observably closer than in most forms of human endeavor. It doesn't take a census to reveal that a large number of successful political leaders live varied and colorful sex lives; much of the language is sexually oriented; political campaigning would be prohibitively expensive were it not for the men and women who volunteer their services for little or nothing in adoration for the candidate or one of his top aides. In Washington, the sexual mores of a Truman, a Nixon, or a Carter — men with a reputation for strict monogamy — are more likely to be the subject of gossip than those of presidents who "play around." There is a tacit, and quite possibly unjustified, assumption that the latter condition is normal.

Personally, I believe that the relationship is inherent in the nature of the profession. There are many definitions of politics, which may or may not be valid depending upon the context in which they are to be used. But in the nation's capital, one definition that is always valid is a description of the political process as: Who does what to whom and when. Of course, many men restrict such activity to the political arena. In the Lyndon Johnson era, macho was the order of the day and the sexual analogue was impossible to avoid.

Johnson was not a man to sublimate his macho instincts. They were well developed. I doubt the suggestion of one of his aides during the White House period that he had "extra glands." But all of the external evidence suggests that those he had were in good working order and frequently exercised. Boudoir activity in which I was not involved has never interested me and I do not intend to pursue the whos, the whats, or the whys. Undoubtedly, the passing of the years will produce considerable literature on that subject, as he was rather open about it. The reigning queen of any given moment was not announced through newspaper advertisements but, short of that, there was little secrecy. I leave the unraveling of what little veil did exist to others.

I am interested, however, in the impact of women on Lyndon Johnson's career and the light his escapades shed upon his life. He did not, as do most politicians, take what was offered and go on to the next bunk. Instead, he found deep meanings in relationships which were often trivial and sometimes with females who can be described as second-rate only through the utmost exercise of charity. When it came to women, he rarely showed the good taste and judgment that he exhibited in his marriage.

The fundamental problem was that Johnson thought women could be trusted just because they were women. He felt they were incapable of deceit unless they were fighting for "my man." To compound his naiveté even further, he believed that any man-woman relationship — sexual, familial, social, or economic — created an enduring bond. His view of the female role in society was not very flattering. They justified their existence as bed mates, cooks, housekeepers, mothers, and secretaries — with the last category at the top of the scale. The greatest destiny he could assign to a woman was that of helpmate to a dominant male.

To those who did not share his outlook, it was startling to hear him refer to some "Dumb Dora" type as "my top assistant." It was more startling, however, to realize that her job was to type some of his letters, route some of his incoming and outgoing mail flow, and soothe his battered ego by bringing him hot coffee (which was never hot enough) — and other comforts. Much of the time, most of the real secretarial work was performed by women with a much higher intelligence quotient but a much lower display quotient. He liked his females spectacular — not just pretty.

LBJ was one of history's most illustrious victims of the Victorian model of women who succeeded in dominating men by displaying

their purity and their weakness. He had been taught by his mother —
a virtual caricature of Victorian toughness hidden under lace — that
the male character was coarse and degraded and redeemable only
through the love and affection of a "good woman." Females, on the
other hand, were characterized by compassion, honesty, tenderness,
and an overwhelming desire to comfort men (who, after all, were
really just grown up little boys). To the modern generation, this may
sound like a clip out of a "camp" movie but it was the prevailing
philosophy of Johnson's boyhood and young manhood. In most parts
of the nation, it had begun to curl around the edges in the early
twenties — but not in Johnson City, Texas.

A more accurate description of his mother would include such
adjectives as tough, stern, unyielding, obstinate, domineering. She
was an unrelenting snob who reminded everyone in the first few
minutes of a meeting that her ancestry included high-ranking Baptist
clerics and intellectuals. She obviously thought she had married
beneath her social rank. Every tour of Johnson City conducted by
someone who knew the family led to a discussion of the "him and her"
doors to the Johnson house. The two, it was explained, had reached a
point where they were not even speaking to each other and needed
separate exits and entrances.

The most dramatic revelation of her character and what she had
done to him came to me one evening when we were driving around
the ranch with some television and news executives whom Johnson
regarded as friends. With one exception, they were non-Texans and
Johnson decided to give them a taste of "Western life." On such
occasions, he would handle his automobile (usually a Lincoln Continental) like a cutting horse — scooting across open country at top
speeds; dodging rocks and clumps of cactus; splitting small herds of
cattle; and fording creek beds which, in that part of the world, were
invariably dry. LBJ ranged far and wide that evening — a beautiful
bend in the Pedernales River; the family cemetery; the house where
he had been born (or thought he had been born); the schoolhouse
where he first learned his ABC's; the high water bridge and the low
water bridge; and a ritualistic stop to see his cousin Oriole. He lapsed
into a reminiscent mood, repeating lines I had heard many times
before about "three generations along the banks of the Pedernales";
the place "where I first discovered America"; "the Johnsons, the
DeShas and the Baines I will join in the cemetery." That night,
however, he opened up a theme I had not heard previously. It was

the courtship of his mother by his father. The key sentence was: "And then that rough, mountain man took that sweet, gentle, cultured woman and brought her up here to live in the lonely hills."

My first reaction was that I must be dreaming. The adjective "cultured" was appropriate — in fact, she was a culture-vulture if one were willing to include in the category of culture such literary masterpieces as "The Boy Stood on the Burning Deck." But "sweet" and "gentle" would have been more appropriately applied to Jesse James or Billy the Kid. She was a formidable woman with a sense of grievance against a destiny that had assigned her to the earthy society of the Texas hill country. I did not know the father who had died long before I became acquainted with LBJ. But the picture I had from talking to people who remembered him did not paint the man as one who could easily bend such a termagant to his will.

The conversation continued and it became plain that I was *not* dreaming. He actually thought his mother a paragon of compassion and tenderness — a haven of safety in a forbidding world. He was willing to accord the quality of political shrewdness to his father who served in the Texas legislature during World War I, but obviously saw him a ruffian whose oldest son had to atone for the indignities that had been visited upon the female parent.

In fact, he did very little atonement when her back was turned. As a rule, his language was colorful, pointed, and what can most charitably be described as "earthy." His "humor" was based chiefly on the contents of toilet bowls and he was addicted to "pie-in-the-face" practical jokes. His favorite spectator sport was watching bovine copulation and he gloried in summoning fastidious males to his bathroom, where conference and excretion could be intermingled. His consumption of beverage alcohol was for purposes other than sacramental and in quantities that did not accord with St. Paul's "a little wine for thy stomach's sake." All of these activities would have offended her Baptist instincts had she known about them, but they were all secondary to his ultimate apostasy — joining the Christian Church during a revival meeting. He claimed later that this was the outcome of a youthful love affair but it is impossible to avoid the suspicion that it was a gesture of rebellion.

Regardless of the scarcity in acts of contrition for his lapses, his mother's viewpoint permeated his life. It governed his relations with the opposite sex, even though those relations took some turns that would have horrified her. During his career, literally thousands of women were greeted with the remark: "You remind me of my mother!" At first I thought it was just a "line" and in most instances it may have been, as it was a not infrequent prelude to intimacy. As time went on, I had to modify that theory. The remark was made to too many women of all ages, shapes, and sizes. Some were very old; some were very young. Some were blonde; others brunettes or redheads. Sometimes they were buxom and cuddly; sometimes they were lean and mysteriously aloof. The only common denominator was an apparent absence of ties to another male — and, even here, there were a few exceptions to the rule.

Naturally, very few of these encounters amounted to more than a ride around the ranch or the privilege of holding his hand while he talked to other people. One of the more famous episodes of his early presidency — speeding through the country roads and drinking beer out of a can while admiring female correspondents in the automobile cooed at him — had its origins with that remark. It was not an invariable prelude to seduction but more of a heartfelt wish. I was struck occasionally by the thought that he was trying to crawl back into the womb.

When his considerations about women involved nonfilial emotions, he had some qualifications. They had to be young, they had to be cheerful, they had to be malleable, and it helped if they were slightly antagonistic to him at the outset. He dearly loved to convert an anti-Johnson liberal with a slightly plump figure and a dowdy wardrobe into a lean, impeccably clad female whose face was masked in cosmetics and who adored the ground he walked on (or, at least, told him she adored the ground he walked on). To her, he would pour out all his dreams and aspirations in what (as it was described to me later by one woman with a sense of humor) was an incredibly potent monologue. The motif was that he trusted her loyalty and needed her wisdom and she had to come with him to occupy the top spot in his organization. It was an offer rarely refused.

The reality was somewhat different. The best the woman could hope for was a position as his private secretary. She learned very quickly that it was not the post of a top "adviser." He had no respect for the political intelligence of any woman except his wife — and, unfortunately, he usually listened to her only when he had done something stupid and had to find a bail-out maneuver.

There were many compensations for the reigning favorite. She could look forward to travel under plush conditions, attendance at glamorous social functions with the Johnsons (he would always find a "safe" male for an escort), expensive clothes, and frequent trips to New York, where a glamorous make-up artist would initiate her into the mysteries of advanced facial make-up, resulting in cosmetics so lavishly applied that they became a mask. The effect was doll-like rather than erotic, which strengthened my belief that his fundamental interest in females had more to do with display than with passion.

There was real power in her position but it had to be exercised in the same style that characterized Nell Gwynne or Madame DuBarry. LBJ believed in the validity of "feminine intuition" and would take seriously her judgments of friend and foe as long as she expressed them indirectly. If she were sufficiently daring, she could act as gatekeeper to determine which memoranda reached his desk and which vanished along the bureaucratic way. Those who played this game artfully found that it gave them power not only in the sense of influencing LBJ but in terms of influencing male aides who discovered that the fastest road to his personal attention was through the thickets of petticoat politics. One top White House assistant owed at least a part of his eminence to the opportune fact that his mistress shared an apartment with a girl who occupied the top of the totem pole for the time being. It should be added, however, that this was a more important factor in the presidency than in the days of his Senate leadership. Legislative advisers had constant access to him on the Senate floor and could find out quickly when their memos had been misdirected.

Very few reigning favorites were allowed to run the office for any great length of time. One of them, who held his attention longer than the rest and for whom he exhibited some really deep feelings, was married off, probably because a continued relationship was incompatible with the vice presidency.

The others dropped back into a pool known to the male staff members (speaking under their breaths) as "the harem." His greatest joy was traveling with a large number of women over whom he could fuss — buying their clothes, supervising their diets, and admonishing them at every public stop to "put on fresh lipstick." It was quite a show. He may have been "just a country boy from the central hills of Texas" but he had many of the instincts of a Turkish sultan in Istanbul.

The word "harem" is actually a misnomer. Some of the so-called members were really secretaries — women of efficiency and intellect who, if they had been males, would have occupied key positions on his staff. How he retained their loyalty, I will never know. He did not bed them and their board was certainly inferior to that of the favorites. Their pay was inadequate to their talents. They frequently found themselves subordinated to women of far lesser ability or loyalty. They were required to give up their individuality without the compensation of participating in the social whirl. And to survive, they had to be adept at all the advanced stages of inter- and intraoffice politics. He was always uncomfortable with women who did not hide their brains.

The result of all this was an office in a constant state of turmoil. A new reigning favorite meant a period of several weeks in which workable routines would be upset; morale would fall to all-time lows; efficiency would go out the window. Fortunately, there were some factors of stabilization. One was Mrs. Johnson herself, who bore the whole thing with incredible fortitude. Always he came back to her because he needed her. She did have brains; she could be trusted; she would step into the breech at the psychological moment and patch up the gaping wounds he had inflicted upon his supporters. Another source of stability was Walter Jenkins, who had the capacity to "forget" the more stupid orders that had originated in the mind of a would-be Marie Antoinette. Walter's arrest in connection with homosexual activity after Johnson entered the White House could well have been a factor in the deterioration of the administration. His successors either did not — or could not — screen out silly ideas.

The harem intrigue was not the most serious aspect of his mother's influence upon him. Far more important, in my judgment, was the view of Victorian respectability that she had ingrained into him. Men were supposed to be quiet, perfectly groomed, mannerly, dressed like an undertaker officiating at a funeral, and at all times "presenting" themselves to the world in tones of the utmost gentility. The prescription fit Lyndon B. Johnson about the same way formal morning clothes fit Mick Jagger.

I believe this had quite a bit to do with the aura of "snake oil" salesmanship that enveloped him even when he was sincere. He never mastered the art of looking like Sir Galahad *sans peur et sans reproche*. If anything, he would assume an ever more cunning countenance when his heart was really in a project. Part of this, I believe, was because he would, on such occasions, fall back on the kind of elocution his mother told him was essential to noble moments.

In fact, he was not above pretensions which amounted to egregious hypocrisy. His public pronouncements supporting a free press were ludicrous — what he really wanted was freedom to buy up journalists. His espousal of a campaign contribution disclosure act was undertaken primarily to ward off the possibility that he would be blamed for some ham-handed efforts by the oil industry to buy votes on a natural gas bill. His widely heralded burning desire to explore outer space evaporated as soon as polls registered a decline in public interest and his assistants had to finish the job. To him, most of these issues were just "hot air" and his true thoughts seemed to surface no matter what he said.

On the stump, the air of contrivance vanished. He could talk to "the folks" and they would believe him. He spoke their language and he came across as "one of us." But the presence of a television camera or a hint of formality undid the picture immediately. He became, on the spot, the little boy who had been taught to recite patriotic poetry at the age of five and it was no longer cute.

It is intriguing to speculate on what would have happened had he still been around when the women's movement began to gather real strength. I personally doubt whether he could have mastered it. He understood the plight of blacks, Chicanos, and poor Appalachians because he could see himself in those terms. But as far as women were concerned, he believed they had "made it" already. Every female problem, in his mind, would be solved by giving their husbands well-paid work. He was determined to give every male good jobs and therefore he regarded himself as the true female benefactor.

During his presidency, he staged a show of high-ranking positions for women. But his heart was not truly in it and the posts were not really very high ranking. This would have been beyond him. Fundamentally, he regarded women as sanctuary. The continued identification of every female with his mother; the obvious security he felt in their presence; his naive, almost infantile, trust in women — these were all of a piece. He was seeking a haven that he never found. Perhaps the reason he needed that haven — which we can never know with certainty — may be the real key to this sorely troubled man.

5

Heroes

Publicly, Lyndon B. Johnson acknowledged three lifetime heroes. They were Alvin Wirtz, a central Texas lawyer who was his patron during his younger days; Speaker Sam Rayburn, who was a propelling force in his rapid rise as a member of the House of Representatives; and Franklin D. Roosevelt, who, he said on every appropriate occasion, had been "like a daddy to me." Privately, he acknowledged another hero — Huey P. Long. But this was something he mentioned only in a circle of very trusted friends. His liberal colleagues had nothing but an occasional glimpse of this affinity. It usually came out when they were discussing Huey, or his brother Earl, in pejorative terms to be interrupted by LBJ with the terse statement: "Don't forget, the Longs never niggered it" (a Southern expression to describe politicians who achieved office by playing on racial tensions).

They were a strangely assorted group. I never met Alvin Wirtz, who died before I joined the Johnson staff. But from those who did know him, I got an impression of an eminently sensible man who combined judgment plus depth of thought. Rayburn I did know well, and he was a man who was deservedly legendary in his own time for integrity, selflessness, and a simple, direct love of country — virtues that are ascribed to many politicians but that fit very few I have encountered. Roosevelt, even long after he was dead, dominated the life and the thinking of Washington in an all-encompassing sense that applied to few of his predecessors or successors. To everyone in the city during the thirties, the forties, and the fifties he was either hero or demon. No one was neutral. Huey and Earl Long, on the other hand, were the very antithesis of the other three. They were brash, raucous, vulgar leaders who raised more problems than solutions.

For many years, it was difficult for me to understand his admiration for the Longs. Neither Earl nor Huey played any apparent role in Johnson's life, and Russell Long — Huey's son with whom he served in the Senate — was not a particularly close friend. The other three men had been his patrons in times when their friendship and support had an observable impact on his destiny. Wirtz seemed to be his key to a firm base in Texas. Rayburn had taught him the subtleties of legislative politics. Roosevelt had been his entree into the glittering world of the New Deal and its galaxy of brilliant idealists, dazzling intellectuals, and resourceful political operators. These men had guided his footsteps into paths that he might otherwise not have followed. Perhaps he would have become equally prominent in other fields had they not existed. But that can only be supposition. They had a direct responsibility in what he *did* become.

Over a long period, I gradually developed an understanding of his attitude. In a very real sense, Wirtz, Rayburn, and Roosevelt *had* been like fathers. They had lavished a paternal type of devotion upon him — set his goals, fostered his career, taught him the practices of maturity. Most important, they had supplied him with the kind of certainties in life that he so badly needed. His strength was his resourcefulness and his tactical brilliance in finding solutions to problems. His weakness was a lack of a clear, philosophical vision of the universe that could furnish a confident identification of the problems and a strategy to bring stability into the environment. His three heroes performed this service for him — as did Richard B. Russell at a later date. They were men who possessed the type of inner confidence that allowed them to accept ultimate responsibility for decision without wavering. He needed that. He could always figure out how to "do it." The question in his mind was what to do.

His admiration for Huey Long came from a totally different quarter. Fundamentally, it was due to a feeling of kinship with the

Kingfish. In his wildest imagination, he could never picture himself as Wirtz, Rayburn, or Roosevelt. He knew how to *use* all three men to advance his own interests and he never hesitated to do so. But he operated on them in the spirit of a very bright child who has developed techniques for wheedling goodies out of his father but has no illusions as to who is the boss of the family. Huey Long, on the other hand, was a figure with whom he could identify. He was brash as LBJ was brash. He was flamboyant as LBJ was flamboyant. He could talk to rednecks and blacks and Cajuns and make them roar with ecstasy as LBJ could talk to rednecks and blacks and Chicanos and make them roar with ecstasy. Both men gloried in vulgarity. Both men were ingenious. Both men had a warm feeling for the underdog.

I could never agree with LBJ's enthusiasm for Huey Long but in time I came to realize that he saw a different Kingfish than I did. To him, Huey was a champion for people who badly needed a defender. Johnson thought of the Longs in terms of free textbooks for schoolchildren; farm-to-market roads; a better break for widows and orphans. He gloried in the announcement Huey made when he decided to go to Arkansas and campaign for Hattie Caraway against an established politician who wanted her Senate seat. "I'm going up to Arkansas and get that big bully off that poor old woman's back," Long said (at least in the LBJ version). Above all, LBJ liked to reminisce over the way Huey had cowed the oil companies in Louisiana. Naturally, this was not mentioned very often in the presence of Texas friends.

Both Johnson and Long would have been superb Jacobin leaders had they lived in France at the time of the revolution. They were men with a deep sense of historic wrongs unaccompanied by deep concepts of how they could be righted.

Johnson, however, had an extra quality which I believe took him above the level of demagoguery and gave him that touch of greatness which was lacking in the Louisiana dictator. LBJ sensed that the world was too complex to be treated as a simple question of punishing wrongdoers and raising the lower part of the masses to the top of the heap. He knew that he needed the presence of men of the Wirtz-Rayburn-Roosevelt stature. And one of the problems of the presidency is that it is an office where a man — at least a man of Johnson's strength — cannot have a patron. The president of the United States can have all the advisers and aides that the society can afford. He is still on his own. He must be his own patron. Under the circumstances, the natural LBJ inclination was to model himself on the one patron who had been president — Franklin D. Roosevelt. It is something of a paradox that his efforts to follow in the footsteps of his hero contributed to a considerable degree to his presidential troubles.

The problem arose out of a psychological quirk that plagued LBJ throughout his life. It was his inability to understand other human beings except in terms of himself — which meant in terms of action. At heart, he was a tactician who had no peer in subtlety when it came to laying plans and devising campaigns. Had he opted for a military career, he would have followed in the tracks of General Patton — rash, swashbuckling, a master of the lightning thrust and capable of taking virtually impregnable military objectives with forces numerically inferior to those of the defense. No one accused General Patton of being a strategist. It was necessary for the United States to use military minds of a different sort to set priorities and to determine the ultimate goals that Patton should achieve. To understand LBJ, this is a distinction that must be borne in mind.

For most of his career, his tactician's outlook presented no handicap. The overwhelming majority of politicians *are* tacticians, rather than strategists, simply because of the requirements of their trade. In the United States they must serve a bewildering array of constituents with highly diverse approaches to the issues of the day. They are required to deal with a broad range of controversies upon only one or two of which they can possibly have expert judgment but upon all of which they must draw authoritative conclusions. This is a way of life that places a high premium on mental agility and verbal nimbleness and tends to eliminate reflective men and women who spend time pondering ends and means.

In this milieu, Lyndon B. Johnson was supreme. No one had more — if as much — mental or verbal agility and he could measure within a micro-millimeter the exact point at which his colleagues would move in the direction he desired. His preeminence in the Senate had little or nothing to do with the proverbial arm twisting. It was fundamentally a capacity to outthink the other senators tactically and to set up issues in such a way that they found themselves incapable of voting against him. Some of these techniques will be discussed in a later chapter. Significantly, during his Senate years he enjoyed the patronage of two very remarkable men who *were* strategists at a very high level and who were determined to do whatever they could to propel LBJ into the presidency. They were Russell and Rayburn.

These two men — the most underrated in written political history
— *could* think long thoughts and *could* set strategic goals. In their
closing years, those long thoughts involved finding means to heal the
warfare between the North and the South, and both settled upon
Johnson as the best vehicle to bring the country to a solution. They
reasoned that his geographical origins would make him acceptable to
the South, despite his lack of "Southern" convictions, and that his
voting record was sufficiently "moderate" to win acceptance in the
North, providing he could be instrumental in finding some solution to
the civil rights controversy.

The impact of these two men in pushing Lyndon Johnson into the
White House deserves considerable elaboration. Unfortunately,
neither could give him advice once he became president. Rayburn
had died and Russell had too much respect for the presidency. (He
once told me: "George! I cannot talk to a president the way I can talk
to a senator" — the most revealing statement I ever heard about the
presidency.) LBJ was forced to play the double role of strategist and
tactician without them. He naturally fell back upon FDR — his
youthful hero.

Unfortunately, what had stamped itself upon his mind most vividly
was the nonstop, whirling action that characterized the Roosevelt
White House. He looked upon it as an incubator in which very young,
very eager, and very ambitious men sat up nights, hatching "ideas"
they could lay upon FDR's desk the next morning. He was convinced
that the Rooseveltian place in history was due entirely to this frenetic
swirl, all of which redounded to the credit of the man in the Oval
Office. This, in Johnson's mind, was the model of the presidency he
should emulate, and he attempted to follow it in every detail. What
emerged was a caricature — a grotesque and very unattractive scene
which, at best, resembled the dances in the Hall of the Mountain
King in *Peer Gynt*.

Those who were in the Johnson administration during the early
days will always think of the White House as an indoor stadium
hosting a perpetual track meet. The halls were the scenes for sprint
after sprint as fleet-footed messengers dashed to bring the latest
bulletin or memorandum to their superiors and sometimes to "the
Chief" himself. The LBJ couriers had a distinctive style, however,
that differed considerably from that of professional athletes. In the
first place, they were completely dressed, including a spotless tie, a

freshly laundered shirt, knife-edge creases in their trousers, and shoes polished to a high gloss. In the second place, their bodies were tilted slightly forward and when they stopped too abruptly, they had a tendency to fall on their faces. Third, they always carried a piece of paper clutched in the right hand — even if they were only on a trip to the mess. Only the president himself dared to walk through the corridors emptyhanded. For anyone else, it was either a confession of impotence or a gesture of defiance.

How close a resemblance this bore to the Rooseveltian model, I do not know. That was before my time. But I have known quite a few New Dealers and I suspect there were some important differences. For one thing, I have an impression that the frantic youths around FDR had to produce something besides quantities of paper or be dropped from the charmed circle. More important, FDR had with him at all times men of seasoned judgment through whom he would filter the stream of "ideas" pouring in from every direction. In my memory, the New Deal was highly pragmatic but it did not indulge in action solely for the sake of action. An idea either bore a direct relationship to a current political problem or it was dropped.

In the Johnson White House, these circumstances did not prevail. The memo artists were judged by quantities of proposals and even those that had to be discarded still scored points for the writer in LBJ's mind. As for men of seasoned judgment, they were usually called in much too late to give him the kind of advice he needed — a systematic approach to the problems of the United States and a listing of priorities. Those who tried to do so without invitation received short shrift. There was no reward for explanations or analysis. Johnson regarded proposals as individual rounds of ammunition and he saw no reason why some should be fired and some should be withheld. Furthermore, he enjoyed springing surprises on the press and public and from long experience he knew that he had to fire fast for surprise because nothing known to three or more men in Washington for any length of time can be kept out of the newspapers. This tendency led to some of his most embarrassing moments — such as his State-of-the-Union proposal to amalgamate the Commerce and Labor departments. He kept it to himself up to the very last minute, so it gave him the headline he was seeking. However, as any one of a number of his friends could have told him had he asked, it was an idea which could not be carried out and which had to be quietly dropped after a few weeks. Only the high regard in which he was held by labor chieftain George Meany saved him from an open and bitter clash with the AFL-CIO.

In the early days of his administration, there was a point to activity for the sake of activity. His constant bombardment of Congress with presidential messages and his continual announcements of presidential action served to reassure the public that Oswald had only killed the president and not the presidency. Americans needed a visible presidency and they got it — even though a disproportionate amount of the visibility consisted of press releases, press conferences on haystacks and other odd places, and long walks on the south grounds of the White House trailed by sweating, miserable journalists and deliriously happy tourists who, to the horror of the Secret Service, had been invited wholesale through the gates.

At first, it was exhilarating. The sensation of action was contagious and reporters relished the flood of news pouring out of the Oval Office. They were fascinated by this stormy, unpredictable character out of the rugged hill country of Texas with his uncanny mastery of Congress and his seeming ability to overcome the most perplexing of problems and to draw the teeth from the most perilous of crises. A civil rights bill — going beyond the wildest dreams of the NAACP — passed the Congress followed by Medicare and a spate of social legislation. A Cuban challenge to the presence of the American Navy in Guantanamo Bay vanished into thin air; an outburst of flame in Panama was dampened down overnight by a series of telephone calls to the president of that country; a head-to-head clash between the right and the left in the Dominican Republic was transformed into the first free election held in the memory of most of its inhabitants.

But the point finally arrived where the process grew thin. It became apparent that much of the motion was simply for the sake of the motion and that frequently it was not even motion but pure razzle-dazzle. Sometimes, the rhetoric obscured genuine achievement of the highest order, as happened in the instance of the Dominican Republic. There was probably no better planned or better managed foreign policy move in Johnson's entire career. When the fighting broke out on the tiny Caribbean island, LBJ succeeded in securing the cooperation of the Organization of American States — which, in practice, meant that U.S. Marines could be landed under the name of an international peacekeeping force rather than as an imperialistic expedition. Once the marines were ashore, their sole role was to keep the left and the right separated and to restore order. Once order was restored, the outcome was a free election won by a man who could not by any stretch of the imagination be considered a friend of the United States.

There was only one trouble. LBJ made himself the only spokesman for the entire operation and, as such, produced a series of explanations for what he was doing that were so incredible the word preposterous would be a kindly epithet. He pictured a total reign of anarchy with the American ambassador hiding under his desk to duck bullets coming into the embassy window. He spoke of several thousand bodies minus heads found under a bridge in the interior, and by his account there appeared to be more Communists on the island than could be found in Moscow's Red Square on May Day.

Some of the stories came from a newly appointed head of the CIA. It turned out that the ambassador had merely told LBJ during a phone call that the embassy window was open and he could hear the shooting in the city of Santo Domingo. But other stories — particularly the headless bodies — could never be traced. I believe that they arose out of his apprehensions for Latin American reaction to the landing of the marines — a force detested by our Spanish neighbors even more than the CIA. He was determined to find palatable excuses for using armed force, and when he was in such a mood, he was invariably ready to believe and state anything — no matter how far-fetched — and even when he had invented it himself. The origin of his statements, however, is not as important as their impact. Too many of them were easily disprovable and, in the eyes of the press, he became a man who had to be observed with a high degree of skepticism.

The incredible frenzy of explanations that enveloped his relatively simple and straightforward action in the Dominican Republic, however, was not the only mischief of his lust for activity. More important, his incessant drive for more projects, more proposals, more laws, actually flawed the enormous body of welfare, social, education, and civil rights legislation upon which he based his hopes for a permanent place in history. In private conversations, he often told his friends that he wanted to be known as "the education president" and that next to that epithet, he would like to be known as "the president for the people." Had legislative volume alone been sufficient, he would unquestionably have earned both titles. But there was too much for society to digest.

At this point of his administration advice from Russell might have made a tremendous difference — not only to the Johnson career but to the presidency and the country as a whole. The Georgia senator, who had a profound understanding of the "Golden Mean" set forth by the Greek philosophers, had been able to damp down some of the Johnson activism in the Senate. He once told me that he believed the nation would benefit if Congress were to restrict its legislative activities to one session every ten years when it should meet to "pass everything in sight." In between, he said, there should be one sitting a year for the appropriation bills. When I expressed dubiety over such a system, he patiently explained to me that a bill was nothing "but a hunting license" for people in the executive agencies to "do good." It takes at least two years — by his estimate — for the administrators to work out practical methods of using the grant of legislative authority. Should the terms of the grant be changed, they must scrap their plans and start all over again. And should the terms be changed too many times in too short a period, the administrators are obliged to spend so much time revising their organizations that they never have time to "do good."

Obviously it is not possible — or even desirable — to restrict Congress to one legislative session every ten years. I have no doubt that Russell, when he was talking to me, had his tongue somewhat in his cheek. But only somewhat. It is possible to pass so many bills on the same subject that action becomes impossible. This was a lesson that Johnson never learned and it was his greatest weakness in comprehending the processes of government. He understood consensus leadership and was as skillful at building coalitions as his idol Franklin D. Roosevelt. He knew how to blunt crises and how to steer militant leaders from arenas of head-on collisions to tables where they could make a deal. Despite the mythology to the contrary, his knowledge of world affairs equalled that of any other president and his instincts were frequently superior to those of the "foreign policy establishment" which grew out of academic participation in World War II. He could extract almost any law he desired from Congress and he had the knack — indispensable to a politician — of making the voters feel he was "one of us." But the Johnsonian range of knowledge did not include any respect for the requirements of orderly administration. In fact, he did not even feel sympathy for it. He was the very antithesis of organized application of the law.

Lyndon B. Johnson really did believe that passage of a bill was full achievement of a goal. He was the epitome of the superstition —

especially widespread among populists and liberals but reasonably common to all Americans — that for every social ailment there is a self-acting legislative nostrum. In his mind, the passage of an antipoverty bill should cure poverty; the passage of an education bill should cure illiteracy; the passage of a civil rights bill should prevent injustice from keeping minorities in bondage. To some extent, this was a heritage from the Roosevelt days when floods of innovative laws put new heart into people and lifted a whole nation out of the doldrums. To some extent, it was a hangover from his days as a congressman when he had always been able to induce bureaucrats to "bend" the rules in gaining favors for his constituents. At most, however, these factors merely reinforced personality traits which were averse to orderly administration.

His senatorial office was a swirling mass of intrigue with the only stabilizing factor his administrative assistant Walter Jenkins. His political campaigns resembled a tornado in intensity and also in unpredictability. He did have a working political organization in every Texas county but that was set up for him by two men who did have a sense of order — Jake Pickle and Cliff Carter — and it was sustained only because he left them alone to run it. Of course, a Texas political organization was of no use to him in the White House and it was abandoned completely. He did place Carter in the Democratic National Committee but restricted his activities so severely that Cliff's natural organizing talents had no opportunity to be tested on a national scale.

Occasionally, the LBJ energy would lead him to intervene in the internal administration of his wife's radio station KTBC (later KTBC-TV). It really was hers and even in a community-property state he had no right to do so. But no one would seriously have considered stopping him even on occasions when the intervention brought the station close to disaster. That happened frequently. He was capable of brilliant conceptions in programming and advertising. But his presence shook the entire staff and often brought key personnel to the verge of a mass walkout. Fortunately, these spurts did not last long. Mrs. Johnson would stand by patiently until his enthusiasm had evaporated and then step back in to soothe ruffled feathers and reinstitute sensible procedures. She *did* have a feeling for orderly administration as well as a solid supply of common sense.

The lesson that Johnson had failed to learn from FDR was that an activist administration needed activist leaders as well as "idea men."

He did not have around him men like Harry Hopkins, Harold Ickes, Bill Douglas of the SEC, or David Lilienthal of the Tennessee Valley Authority. I suspect that some of his cabinet officers were capable of playing similar roles but they never got the chance. They were kept too busy pushing new bills, new approaches, new panaceas dreamed up by the staff in the White House, which had discovered early in the administration that the road to presidential favor was paved with proposals. They turned out more than the heads of the large agencies could possibly digest while keeping their own staffs under control.

Any effort to discuss this problem with him received curt treatment. He simply was not interested. He recalled too vividly the days when he could get favors — as a congressman — out of agency heads and thought this meant that the agencies could operate without top supervision or method. He never understood the difference between individual cases handled by legislators and large-scale application of the law. The one area of administration to which he paid attention was the preparation of the budget. Here, however, he was too interested in the impact of the *figures* upon the public to pay attention to other implications. He relished for years one situation in which he persuaded the press that only a miracle would keep the document below $100 billion. At the last moment, he produced the miracle (which had, unknown even to most members of his staff, been up his sleeve all the time) and accepted the plaudits of the nation. The act grew mighty thin after the first exhibition but he kept on trying it out, year after year, just the same.

What was much more serious was the lid placed upon his domestic programs by the spending for the war in Vietnam. No one will ever know the exact cost of that military effort because no rule exists for sorting out the money spent in Southeast Asia from the money spent for general defense. But the ambitious programs of what LBJ called "the Great Society" were not backed by dollars correspondingly as ambitious. The result was an *appearance* of social change but very little social change outside of the appearance. To his credit, Johnson did not try to pretend that he was supplying the money. What he said was that the programs had to be deferred pending the Vietnamese war. The problem with his explanation was that it was not widely heard or understood by the public.

What really happened is that expectations were raised to tremendous heights. The blacks, the Chicanos, the people left in economic deadends in Appalachia thought that major assistance was on the way.

Middle-class whites thought that "everything was being done for the minorities." Actually, nothing was being "done" except the passage of laws, and it may well be that the tensions of recent years have been exacerbated by the feeling of minorities that they have been sold down the river again and of the white middle class that the minorities are "ungrateful" for all the "favors" they have received. Many of the laws, of course, were boons to middle-class blacks who needed no economic help but who found social barriers lowered to them. Most blacks, however, still live in slums and their right to eat in elegant Washington restaurants is somewhat hollow.

The social legislation is still on the books. Perhaps some future president will be able to use the authority to change society. But at best this will be deferred achievement. Converting the authority into practical programs will be much more difficult than the original task of securing the authority itself. First, someone must take a look at what has been done to determine what is usable and what should be discarded. In the present climate, which is breeding distaste for social engineering, this will not be a simple task. Perhaps it would have been simplified had not Johnson's hero worship for FDR resulted in a grotesque caricature of the New Deal White House.

6

A Philosophy of Life

Lyndon Johnson once described to me a philosophy of human growth in which life was divided into three periods. The first was one in which a man or woman prepared for what was ahead. The second consisted of a struggle for achievement. The third was a time in which the achiever relaxed and enjoyed the fruits of the victories. I do not know whether he really believed in this progression or whether it was just another aphorism he picked up from a speechwriter. Nevertheless, it is obvious that he followed this pattern up to middle life. And it may well be that his erratic behavior in the late fifties, when the presidency became a distinct possibility for him, can be traced to the realization that he had been betrayed by this outlook on existence. He discovered too late that learning, doing, and enjoying should be, if at all possible, mixed into every day.

Like everything else about the man, this can only be an inference from the facts. He was rarely candid, and when he spoke of personal matters his words were such a mixture of fantasy, euphemism, and half-truth that it was impossible to separate out the nuggets of revelation. In this case, however, the facts are compelling. As it became clearer that inexorable forces were pushing him into the small circle of men from whom the nation picks its chief executives, he developed a pattern of conduct that indicated beyond a doubt a desire to revert to childhood. He intermingled, almost daily, childish tantrums; threats of resignation (which I realize in retrospect were the equivalent of the small boy who says he will take his baseball and go home); wild drinking bouts; a remarkably nonpaternal yen for young girls; and an almost frantic desire to be in the company of young people. It was an obvious search for a wasted youth.

He did not wear the mantle of age with any grace because he had never learned to enjoy anything but sensual activity. He could think but not reflect; devise ingenious schemes for achieving goals but not ponder the validity of the goals; outguess his fellow human beings in playing the great game of one-upsmanship without realizing that the game might not be worth playing. In short, he had none of the contemplative qualities which, in old age, can compensate for the loss of youthful vigor. A few weeks after his heart attack in 1955, he summed up the whole problem when he told a conference of doctors, gathered to evaluate his condition, that he enjoyed nothing but whiskey, sunshine, and sex. Without realizing what he was doing, he had outlined succinctly the tragedy of his life.

The doctors had prepared both the family and the intimate staff for changes in his character and for conduct that would seem to be irrational. But nothing they said gave us a real foretaste of the intensity with which he manifested his inner turmoil. It would not be accurate to say that his personality *changed*. Everything he did was foreshadowed by traits which had become apparent in his earlier life. But before the heart attack his darkest side was kept under a modicum of control. After the heart attack, he stopped short only of supreme disaster — and not very short of that. Sometimes it seemed as though he really wanted to get caught doing something outrageous so he would no longer have to make decisions or accept responsibilities.

The drinking bouts became increasingly heavy and increasingly frequent. When he was with staff members, there would usually be a point at which he would launch a tirade reviling an assistant for a long series of fancied wrongs and assumed inadequacies. He did not do this with younger members of the staff. He would assemble with them in the evening — especially in Texas when the Senate was out of session — and spend hours basking in their company, obviously at peace with the world and forgetful that dinner was waiting for him at home as well as a frantic wife. At other times, when he was with his peers, he would threaten to walk out on his current position.

Why the members of his staff stuck with him — including me — is a question I cannot answer to this day. It had something to do with a feeling that he was a truly great man and that we owed it to the country to put up with his rampages so he would be there when he was needed. The sentiment may sound squishy to those who have never been close to him but he was capable of generating incredible loyalty. Naturally, we put the best face on things that we could. We ascribed his tantrums to an inferiority complex. This gave us a feeling that at heart he was a modest man, unaware of his great gifts. In fact, he did have an inferiority complex. It was not, however, the whole explanation for the conduct of a very complicated man.

Nowhere did this inferiority trait surface more readily than his oft repeated threats to quit whatever responsibility he held at the time and relinquish the field to someone else. Those were terrible moments for the audience — usually small and very select. It took me some time to realize that they fell into a pattern which itself had some significance. They were invariably preceded by a wild drinking bout. He was not an alcoholic or a heavy drinker in the commonly accepted sense of those words. But there were occasions when he would pour down Scotch and soda in a virtually mechanical motion in rhythm with the terrible tension building visibly within him and communicating itself to his listeners. The warning signs were unmistakable and those with past experience tried to get away before the inevitable flood of invective. As they found out, it was rarely possible.

There did not appear to be any relationship between the locale and the episode. It could happen in his Capitol office; in the living room of his ranch; in a tourist court on a campaign swing. But invariably those upon whom it was inflicted were people who held him in personal affection; invariably it took place at a moment when to carry out the threat of resignation would have had a disastrous effect upon some major enterprise; always it was the prelude to a major triumph which raised him even higher in public esteem. Invariably also, he would arise the next morning calm, cool — acting as though there had been no such episode and, naturally, no one would remind him of it. I sometimes wondered whether the whole thing was not an act of propitiation — an assurance to the gods that he was aware of his unworthiness and sought their help.

Early in our relationship, I became somewhat inured to this phenomenon. The last time I took it seriously during his congressional days was when he launched into the threat during a drinking bout in the office of the secretary of the Senate. On that particular night, the Republican floor leader, Senator William Knowland of California, was present and it seemed to me that Johnson would not say such things before a member of the opposition party unless he really meant them. What I had not realized up to that time was that Knowland — despite ideological and political differences — held LBJ in such high regard that he merely joined the Democratic senators who were present in begging him to change his mind. Apparently, Knowland's entreaties were successful. A smiling Johnson showed up on the Senate floor the next day and organized a coup that wound up with the Democrats seeming to rescue a Republican president (Eisenhower) from the machinations of conservative Republican senators.

As the 1960 campaign drew closer, the drinking bouts surpassed all previous records. They also coincided with a shrinking away from all of his old comrades who might have mounted a substantial thrust for the Democratic nomination. Men like Tom Corcoran and Jim Rowe found it increasingly difficult to catch his ear. One by one, the stalwarts of the New Deal went to other candidates until virtually no big names were left in his camp. At the same time, however, he refused to cut off all prospects of striving for the nomination. His staff members were bewildered by his conduct. He was repelling substantial help but he refused to slam the door. He was obviously torn between a desire to fling away his political career and enjoy a second youth and a realization that the great prize was within his reach if he only made the effort. The result was that he merely looked ludicrous.

Nevertheless, his position in the Democratic Party was so strong that he could not be denied the nomination for the vice presidency. He had kissed his chance for a second youth goodbye. He did not do so easily. The 1960 campaign was a nightmare for the staff — a weird collage of beratings, occasional drunken prowls up and down hotel corridors, and frantic efforts to sober him up in the mornings so he could make speaking engagements. Here again he came close to disaster. He spent a whole night in a hotel room in El Paso pouring invective upon the head of a bewildered advance man. He could just barely see when Jack Kennedy joined us the next morning. It was to be a joint appearance and how he carried it off, I will never understand. It was a day in which we had to lead him by the hand. Even so, his speeches were effective.

Strangely enough, he was effective throughout the campaign. There is little doubt in my mind that he delivered the margin of victory. His train trip through the South was a triumph and salvaged states that otherwise would have gone to Richard M. Nixon. His automobile tour through the coal regions of Pennsylvania stirred real enthusiasm. And his appearance before the Liberal Party in New York was spectacular. On the stump he had very few peers. But in his rooms at night, the drinking patterns continued as did the threats of leaving the campaign.

Despite these and other experiences, however, I was not prepared for the climactic resignation threat made to me, personally, in 1964, the night before he flew to Atlantic City to accept the Democratic presidential nomination. We had worked quite late in the White House that night but he kept me even later than the rest of the staff. Sometime around midnight, he asked me to go with him for a walk on the south lawn. It was then that he told me he intended to appear before the Democratic convention and withdraw his name from nomination. Nobody, he said, really wanted him; the heart and soul of the Democratic Party was with Bobby Kennedy; blacks would not vote for him; liberals thought he was just a tobacco-chewing Southerner; there was nothing left for him to do but go back to Texas and spend the rest of his days along the banks of the Pedernales, "which has been the only home where Johnsons are appreciated."

There was something terribly convincing about him and my cynicism evaporated quickly. His reasoning bore only the faintest resemblance to reality. Vietnam had yet to intrude on the public consciousness and his popularity was high — not only with the Democratic Party but with Americans generally. Blacks had come to look upon him as a man who carried out his promises; liberals had found that he was far to their left on most issues; everywhere there was an outpouring of gratitude toward this man who had helped the nation recover from the traumatic shock of a presidential assassination. There was little doubt that Bobby Kennedy was thirsting to occupy the White House but LBJ had handled much tougher opposition in Texas under far more unfavorable circumstances. The whole thing was grotesque. To carry out the threat would mean a split in the Democratic Party regardless of who received the nomination. The only conceivable outcome would be a Barry Goldwater triumph.

This was one of the few occasions of my life when I actually panicked. I pleaded with him to change his mind. He said that it was all made up and he wanted me to write his resignation statement. I refused and he replied that he had plenty of writers on the string who would do it for him. I raised the question of Democratic Party demoralization; he said that he had done more for the party than it had done for him. I raised the threat of a Goldwater victory; he said that was preferable to four years of internecine warfare between himself and Bobby Kennedy. I could not shake him. We finally broke it off and I went home to a very sleepless night.

The next day, of course, he flew to Atlantic City and accepted the nomination with every evidence of satisfaction.

He finally did resign but it was an action of a different magnitude. When he made his famous speech withdrawing his candidacy in 1968, it was preceded by no drunken bout; by no abuse of close friends; by no histrionics lasting late into the night. This time he meant it — a fact that inevitably raises the question of what he really meant on all the earlier occasions.

Perhaps the threats were related to another phenomenon — his tendency to fly into rages for reasons totally inadequate to the degree of ferocity which he would display. This was a feature of the vice-presidential years but it was not limited to that period. It was noteworthy that these outbursts would happen often in the presence of people who were not his friends and who could — and probably did — create considerable trouble for him at a later time.

The prime example took place in the Erewon Hotel in Bangkok in 1962 when Johnson had been sent by President Kennedy on a trip through non-Communist Asia. He had been suspicious of the project from the start — regarding it as a Bobby Kennedy "plot" to make him look ridiculous in some foreign nation. (In talking to me, he compared the situation to that in which mobs assailed former Vice President Nixon in Venezuela. "Bobby wants to make me look like Nixon," he would roar.) The president had sent his sister Jean and her husband — Steve Smith — along obviously as an expression of his interest in a part of the world which was highly unstable. LBJ, however, decided that Steve was along as a "spy," and tension began to mount as soon as the presidential plane took off from Washington. The first few nations were unalloyed triumphs from a public standpoint and Johnson began to relax. Cheering crowds had turned out in Vietnam, in the Philippines and on Taiwan. He was in a state of euphoria. The blow fell when we reached Thailand, bringing with us an ambassador newly appointed to that nation.

During the evening, Johnson's elation eroded to be replaced by dark despair and self-pity. He berated the bewildered ambassador for no observable reason other than that he was a Kennedy liberal. He reviewed all the plots against him and, by inference, made the victim of his tirade the bellwether for what he conceived to be the entire Kennedy operation. The ambassador protested that none of this was true — that LBJ was a man beloved by his country and esteemed by his party. The protestations brought an even higher level of self-pity which in turn brought an even higher level of protestation. I have often wondered what kind of report Steve Smith brought back to the White House. He is a gentleman and he may have dismissed the whole thing out of hand. But the most important thing to me that night was the very obvious point of the whole exercise — LBJ was using the evening to draw declarations of affection and loyalty.

From that time on, I thought that the threatened resignations and the furious outbursts were techniques to bolster Johnson's own self-esteem. Otherwise, it seems to me that one of the threats would have been carried out and that the outbursts would not have ended so quickly. It was impossible not to be suspicious when all the circumstances were taken into account. Too many of the wild rages were obviously contrived.

The most vivid example of the controlled outburst occurred in the fall of 1955 when he was recuperating on his ranch from the heart attack. The 1952 Democratic presidential candidate, Adlai Stevenson, was visiting Austin to give a lecture at the University of Texas and, naturally, expressed a desire to pay a courtesy visit to LBJ — then the Senate Democratic leader. The invitation from the ranch was prompt and, when questioned by the press, Stevenson told them of the forthcoming visit. The press called me to find out what the visit was about and when I relayed the calls to Johnson, the storm broke. He promptly took to his bed and fretted and fumed and raised the grim specter of a recurrence of the heart attack. One of my most poignant memories is a call from Mrs. Johnson late in the night pleading with me to keep the press in Austin while Stevenson came to visit her husband. I could only tell her that the ranch itself was private property and the family could exclude anyone but that I could not keep journalists off the public highway which gave access.

Some of the tension communicated itself to the press and to Stevenson, who offered to skip the visit if it would put too much of a strain on Johnson. Obviously, at that point, the meeting could not be dropped from the schedule without raising serious questions as to Johnson's health. The press went out to the ranch in the morning with great apprehension.

The tension was broken immediately. The AP reporter standing at the gate was startled to see Johnson coming toward him in a golf cart. "Are you going to throw me out of Texas, Senator?" he asked. Johnson laughed and invited him for a ride. Other journalists had arrived by that time and a caravan was formed which toured the entire ranch — including the cemetery and the semimythical house in which, LBJ frequently said, "I first discovered America."

The whole day flowed in similar fashion. The ranch tour was repeated for Stevenson's benefit and was followed by a press conference. LBJ was in complete command of the situation and Adlai — to whom I had communicated the tensions that had been created — kept stealing glimpses at me as though I were demented. I hope that later experience illuminated the situation for him.

Why did he do it? Part of it was probably sheer joy over manipulating other people. Part of it was sheer boredom with a medically dictated regimen that did not suit his restless personality. Part of it may have been a simple device to insure the loyalty of his family or associates (after all, we all tried to reassure him of our devotion). But I believe the major part of it was the desire to build a stunted ego. What he had done was to demonstrate to himself once more that he was sufficiently important to induce people to put up with irrational behavior on his part — and that meant he was important indeed.

Obviously Johnson's rages were significant. But significant of what? I believe that to some extent they were a means of controlling people by securing expressions of their loyalty. To some extent they were an expression of an inferiority complex. To some extent, they were a "kicking against the traces" — a rebellious reaction to his lost youth. But I cannot avoid the feeling that there were deeper causes which will probably never be known. Perhaps they were within his genes.

Many years later, I overheard his daughter Lynda Bird expressing some rather juvenile opinions on how *she* handled television interviews. One of the attendants in her vicinity sighed and said: "Lynda Bird! You must *earn* the right to be difficult!" Possibly the final word is that LBJ *had* earned that right and elected to exercise it.

7

A Gap of Understanding

Of all the LBJ weaknesses, perhaps the most important was his inability to understand the press. He was totally baffled by journalists who practiced an art that he regarded as a mystery and he never fully comprehended why they failed to respond to the type of treatment he practiced so successfully on other politicians and on government officials.

Part of his problem arose out of his early experience with the Texas press — an intensely partisan collection of newspapers, many of which opposed him from the start. To the conservative majority of newspapers in the state, he was so far to the left as to be beyond discussion in any terms other than invective. To the few liberal organs, which were as passionate as their conservative counterparts, he was too far to the right to be countenanced. None of them, conservative *or* liberal, paid any attention to the distinction between "straight news" or opinion pieces on the editorial pages. When a Texas journal had a cause, it sailed into the fray money, marbles, and chalk.

Over the years, Johnson managed to soften much of the opposition by forming lasting friendships with Texas publishers. It was a state where publishers maintained the tradition of keeping daily and tight

editorial control over their news columns long after the practice had
disappeared in the North. The shift in some of the newspapers as a
result of his blandishments was little short of amazing. He had
learned the fine art of scaring the conservatives with liberal
bogeymen and the liberals with conservative bogeymen and thus
drew grudging support from both sides. The conservatives, for example, were fed a steady diet on the demise of 27½ percent oil depletion
and the Texas claims to the tidelands if experienced legislative warriors like Johnson and Rayburn were removed from office. The liberals, on the other hand, were startled to find themselves supporting
him because he was the only conceivable alternative to the political
machine fastened upon the state by conservative Allan Shivers. It was
a nimble-footed performance compared to which a pas de deux by
Nijinsky would resemble a Dutch clog dance.

Another part of his problem, however, arose out of his own combative instincts which produced a vision of life as a continuous battle in
which every living soul took part. He once described Washington as a
city in which the key question was, "Who is doing the fucking and who
is getting fucked," and while one of the purposes of the statement was
to shock the immediate audience it was also a good summary of his
political philosophy. To be certain that he was in the first, rather than
the second, category, he polished to a high gloss the technique of the
carrot and the stick. It worked beautifully for most of the Washington
establishment but he never succeeded in adapting it to the press —
chiefly because he did not understand the objectives of journalism.
He and the reporters were not even in the same physical dimension,
let alone on the same wave length.

His early experiences, plus the failures of his "carrot and stick"
efforts, instilled within him a picture of the press which was as
unshakable as it was mistaken. To him, newspapers were arenas in
which contending politicians battled for dominance. The method of
combat was a continuing effort to capture reporters by granting favors
to those who wrote "good stories" and by withholding vital news from
those who were "mean."

Had there been some knowledge of journalistic problems to accompany his philosophy, he might have had a measure of success.
Journalists are neither more nor less honorable than any other group
within our society, and to regard their craft as a higher calling that
precludes venality is far less sensible than belief in the tooth fairy.
There are newspapermen who can be bought and he bought them.

Unfortunately, they were not the most important and he did not know what to do with them after they were bought. Meanwhile, those who were independent but disposed to acknowledge his greatness were invariably sluffed off because he expected them to do things that they simply could not do. He did not realize that stories are usually written because they have happened, and he looked to his journalistic "friends" to ignore or to explain away anything he did not want to see in print.

LBJ's concepts of what should — and what should not — be written frequently prevented the publication of stories he would have liked very much to read. There were journalists in Washington — men of very high standing — whose admiration for him as a political leader was very high. They hesitated, however, to write anything about him that could be interpreted as being "nice" because it might also brand them as trained seals. One reporter, for example — Phil Potter of the *Baltimore Sun* — treated him rudely at every opportunity just so there would be no illusions. On one occasion, Johnson called Phil to say he needed "a certain story written" only to have Phil advise him to call the advertising department. The *Sun* correspondent then hung up the phone while LBJ was still talking. What makes this incident so ironic is that Phil thought he was one of the greatest statesmen of the decade.

To complicate the situation even further, he had absolutely no grasp of the obligation laid upon writers to select adjectives appropriate to the nouns being modified. As far as he was concerned, some adjectives sounded nice and made a good impression upon the readers and some adjectives sounded bad and therefore had the opposite effect. Journalists, he thought, selected descriptive words solely to further a cause to which they were committed or to block a cause to which they were opposed or because they had been hypnotized into using the word by clever public relations types. The hypnosis theory produced some efforts on his part which ran the gamut from ludicrous to grotesque.

For a long time Johnson envied what he regarded as the highly favorable press treatment accorded to Democratic Senator Herbert S. Lehman of New York. He was particularly impressed by the frequency with which journalists coupled the adjective "sincere" with the name Lehman and concluded that this resulted from a heavy investment in public relations. Most of us on the LBJ staff were less than impressed by the same set of facts. It seemed to us that the

Lehman name showed up rarely in the newspapers because he was a very ineffectual senator. He was not a factor in the legislative process (aside from his vote) but he was likable, and when reporters did write something about him they invariably resorted to the "sincere" description. It was not truly a compliment — they just could not think of any other epithet that was true that was not also patronizing.

Reporters did not use the same adjective to describe LBJ because there were so many others that were more appropriate. They thought of him as forceful, commanding, competent — qualities beside which the word "sincere" paled into insignificance even when it was justified. I tried to explain this to him but to no avail. When I refused to undertake a campaign to change the press viewpoint on this matter, he launched his own. Someone had told him about the theories of subliminal conditioning then making the rounds and his methodology was to mutter "sincere" over and over in the presence of journalists. When he could insert the word into a sentence, he would do so even when it had to be dragged in by the heels, kicking and screaming. When he could find no sentence that was suitable, he would repeat "sincere" under his breath, over and over to the absolute bewilderment of his audience. Fortunately, he dropped the effort before articles could appear questioning his sanity.

Unfortunately, he had a highly exaggerated view of the successes with the press achieved by the John F. Kennedy operation. Kennedy was more successful than most but largely because Kennedy knew what was possible and did not try to push journalists into writing stories that they could not write. Had Johnson been able to comprehend the same set of principles, he would have had the press eating out of his hand. It may come as something of a shock to Kennedy backers but almost any writer who had to deal with both men would concede that the Johnson personality was much more fascinating. JFK was glamorous, sophisticated, polished, and vibrant. LBJ did not have those qualities but he was stormy, unpredictable, earthy, and gigantic. Even his most outrageously petty moods had something titanic about them.

The Kennedy success was limited largely to a few columnists who had more of a following inside Washington than they did in the rest of the nation. Johnson, however, saw them as "the press" and concluded — regardless of the evidence — that journalists were against him. He attributed their alleged "opposition" to the "snobbery" of the "Eastern establishment" against a boy from the central hill country of Texas. His inferiority complex operated to its fullest and he interpreted as slights written words which were either trivial or, in some cases, highly favorable.

On his "good-will" tour of Scandinavia, for example, the trip was covered for the *New York Times* by Werner Wiskari, an American-born correspondent of Finnish descent. Wiskari joined the party at Stockholm. Johnson was taken into the city by helicopter from the airport and was greeted upon landing by a group of schoolboys. He said something to them which I could not hear because the helicopter pilot had not shut off his engine but came out in the *Times* the next day as, "How are you guys?" Johnson was furious. He concluded that Wiskari was an "Eastern snob" attempting to portray him as an illiterate who used such gutter language as "guys." I spent the rest of the time in Scandinavia keeping the two men apart while at the same time keeping them sufficiently close that the reporter was not denied the right to coverage.

It was a trip studded with boners. Johnson violated the Scandinavian reverence for punctuality by showing up late for all receptions and made it starkly clear that he was not enjoying his social companions.

He walked across a mass grave at Rovaniemi — where all the populace was massacred during the Russo-Finnish War — to shake hands with Finns startled to see him committing what was to them an act of desecration. Wiskari recorded every such incident. I, myself thought he was leaning over backward to put Johnson's activities in perspective but LBJ interpreted every story as a personal attack. He even insisted that some of the stories were fictitious — especially one about an egg being thrown at him as he entered the hotel at Helsinki. It was possible that he had not seen it and had already gone through the doors. But a number of us had witnessed the incident and talked him out of denouncing the *New York Times* for printing the account.

This occurred when he was vice president and obsessed with the idea that Bobby Kennedy was directing an anti-LBJ campaign. His elevation to the presidency made absolutely no difference. Brush after brush took place with the journalists who, in the early days of his administration, accepted him as a miracle worker to be treated with downright reverence. Eventually, however, his conviction that they were opposed to him created an opposition — always the outcome of paranoia. He did not attribute this to his own shortcomings but to the machinations of the man he regarded as his arch foe. At this stage of the game, Bobby was helpless to do him much mischief but LBJ still believed that there was a plot for which the press was the principal instrument.

This led to some extraordinarily clumsy efforts to revise the rules of White House coverage so he could restrict the range of journalistic activity. One of his worst moves was to abolish the "press pool" which always traveled on the president's airplane. It consisted of one correspondent from each of the two wire services; one correspondent from the radio-TV networks; and one correspondent drawn, under a complicated set of rules, from the general reporters on the trip. The concept of the pool was not one of ordinary press coverage. The reporters were to swing into action only in case of an emergency. The individuals assigned to it really wanted nothing but a chance to relax over a drink while flying between cities.

Johnson refused to accept the obvious fact that this was only "protection" coverage designed to insure the presence of experienced White House correspondents on the scene if something went wrong. He insisted that they were "spies" (his exact word) whose only purpose was to search out embarrassing secrets. He sought to counter the espionage by leaving his cabin and sitting with the reporters throughout the trip, on the theory that he would distract them from pursuing their nefarious schemes. At first, the newsmen were delighted. It was quite an experience for most of them to spend hours in intimate conversation with a president of the United States. After a few weeks, however, their enthusiasm began to pall. For one thing, in his presence they could not indulge in the most favored form of journalistic recreation, which is talking about journalism. For another, sitting with a president is a strain on anyone. And, finally, he eventually ran out of interesting reminiscences and there was no real news — or even titillation — in his garrulous monologue. I tried to convince him that both he and the press would be better off if he stayed in his cabin and left them alone. This merely led to a second stage.

The second stage was an announcement to me that the press pool was to be abolished. He said the idea had been started by Pierre Salinger, at Bobby Kennedy's instigation, and there was no reason why a succeeding regime should not change the rules. I resisted bitterly, pointing out that the pool had been instituted by Jim Haggerty during the Eisenhower regime and that it had become one of the most accepted institutions in the White House. The answer was that I was "naive" and the pools were ended. From there on out, his relationship with the press was one of constant warfare. The "stick" brought him nothing but trouble.

Unfortunately, the "carrot" got him into trouble also. He became too exuberant about entertaining reporters at his ranch under circumstances that threw some irresistible stories in their direction. When the stories were written, he concluded that his hospitality was being abused and that journalists could not be trusted. He was especially bitter over the previously mentioned account of his speeding through the hill country in a Lincoln Continental, one hand on the steering wheel and the other hand clutching a beer can while he cooed softly to a rather toothsome female correspondent. When the story broke, his bitterness knew no bounds. He asked me how to prevent such accounts from appearing and I told him bluntly that there was no way to do it but to leave the correspondents behind and not hit 80 mph or better over the back-country Texas roads.

A much more serious incident, however, involved his Cousin Oriole — an elderly woman who had a few acres adjoining his ranch. She was a colorful personality who lived frontier style in a little shack on her property and her major source of income was rental paid to her by LBJ for pasturing his sheep on her land. After his heart attack in 1955, he had been instructed to walk one mile every evening. In typical LBJ fashion he measured a half mile along the road (on an automobile odometer) from the front of his ranchhouse and discovered that it was just a little short of his cousin's front door. Thus began a standard institution on the ranch — the nightly "walk to see Cousin Oriole." The ritual had a rough-hewn charm to it. As a rule, ten to fifteen people would be involved, all of whom were expected to make as much noise as possible, with the decibels increasing as they came closer to the objective. On the pretext that she was stone deaf (only partially true) Johnson would pound on her door as though his fist were a battering ram breaking down the city gates during a siege. After a suitable interval, Cousin Oriole would come to the front door in her bare feet — pretending indignation but obviously pleased at all the attention. For twenty minutes or so, everyone would crowd into her little house, where LBJ would shout meaningless questions at her about her sheep (she usually heard the word as "sleep" — a factor which enhanced the charm of the occasion) and then everyone would depart leaving behind a thoroughly happy woman.

One night he took a group of correspondents on the expedition and they were enchanted. Helen Thomas of the United Press wrote a piece about it for which any publicity man would pay thousands of dollars. She captured the essence of the occasion — the smell of the frontier; Cousin Oriole's fierce independence; Johnson's rough, but somehow tender, sensitivity to the loneliness of an elderly widow. To me, the piece spelled out "votes" by the millions from Americans still nostalgic for the "good old days" of self-sufficiency and tightly knit families united to ward off the evils of the world. That was not the way Johnson read it. To him, it was a story inspired by Bobby Kennedy with the purpose of telling the United States that the Johnsons were nothing but a tobacco road family whose highest level of literacy was the Sears Roebuck catalogue hanging in the privy. He was particularly incensed by the line on "bare feet" — a phrase he associated with hookworm and pellagra.

The situation was grotesque. It would take a real leap of the imagination to conceive of Helen Thomas as a Kennedy sycophant. To the contrary, her admiration (adoration would be a better word) was directed toward Lady Bird. She had written the story only because it was a good story and would have bitterly — and rightly — resented the implication that it was pro or con anybody. Nevertheless, the president set out to punish her by cutting off all the special "goodies" he reserved for the distaff side of the press. There were no more sessions on the ranch; no more walks on the south lawn in the evenings. This ostracism was something LBJ did on his own cognizance and without consulting anybody. I had been quite blunt to him about his ludicrous interpretation of her story. Helen, however, did not understand and probably blamed me for being cast into outer darkness. That may have explained the enmity toward me which she has nursed over the years.

One or two such incidents would have been bearable. But they kept multiplying. He insisted that I call reporters — and sometimes publishers — to complain about stories and I refused to make such a fool of myself. He personally called one or two and discovered quickly it was not a very good tactic for handling the press. It merely produced more stories about the telephone calls. He finally compromised by finding other White House assistants to register his complaints for him. This made them happy because it was a token of his favorable attitude toward them and they were unaware of the ridiculous posture in which they were being placed. It made Johnson happy because "at least those bastards know what I think of them."

Unfortunately, it produced no difference in the stories that were written and this was more fuel for his paranoia.

After the election of 1964, his obsession with the press mounted to furious heights. Some individual journalists found ways of capitalizing on it. One White House correspondent wangled an informal luncheon with him one day and, in the middle of the conversation, dropped the phrase: "The trouble with the press is that they are a bunch of crybabies." Three days later, his paper appeared featuring a superb selection of photographs that had been taken by the White House photographer. I was left with the press to explain something that could not be explained — why exclusive pictures had been slipped out. I believe that most of them understood my problem. They also understood that to protect themselves they had to connive with White House assistants outside the press office. Johnson was quite pleased with this arrangement as he thought it increased his opportunities to reward "friends" and punish "enemies." It exacerbated the Palace Guard politics which had plagued the White House from the beginning and also permitted a number of his more clever assistants to garner some press coverage for themselves.

Underlying all the other problems, however, was his conviction that reporters were merely transmission belts for shrewd public relations men. He thought that Pierre Salinger had elected John F. Kennedy and that Jim Haggerty was responsible for the esteem in which the nation held Eisenhower. Even his hero — Franklin Delano Roosevelt — in his mind was partially a product of Charley Michelson, the now-forgotten publicity director of the Democratic National Committee who was famous for coining stinging epithets to throw at Republicans. Charley Michelson was before my time but Salinger and Haggerty were, to my knowledge, men of the highest competence. He did not think of them, however, as men of the highest competence but as men who could dictate the front-page stories on most of the newspapers in the United States. It was out of this fantastic belief that he presented me with a demand that was apocalyptic in its sheer looniness. He wanted his press conferences scripted — all the questions and answers written out in advance and then staged before the TV cameras.

I told him "nothing doing" from the start but he kept pressing on the grounds that "Pierre Salinger did it that way." It took me some time to find out the genesis of this amazing belief. It arose from sessions which John F. Kennedy held with his cabinet and with the vice president before every press conference. At those sessions, Pierre (who was fresh from a session with me and top public affairs officers of the government) would read a list of twenty or so questions that would be asked by the press. Invariably, reporters covering the session would ask at least eighteen or nineteen (and usually all twenty). There was no mystery to the matter. Anyone with a reasonable degree of journalistic experience can predict the questions that will be asked at a news conference. It was simply a matter of understanding the flow of news. This Johnson did not understand. He thought that Salinger had "planted" these questions on reporters and that all Kennedy had to do was to recognize those who had agreed to take the plants.

The planted question is an old institution in Washington. But as a rule it was used only when a politician was afraid that the press would *not* ask a question he wished to answer (and did not wish to volunteer the answer but wanted to have it "dragged out" of him) or when the wording of the question would affect the impact of the answer. In those days, a majority of reporters were willing to take an occasional plant and did not regard the practice as imposing any undue obligations on them. However, a press conference resting entirely on "plants" would throw the press into an uproar. It was tried once by one of my successors and the result was exactly what I had predicted.

The tensions between the president and the press continued to mount and as they did, I was suspected of being too "pro press" and too "unimaginative" in my approach. He once explained patiently to me that the job of a press secretary was to think up good stories for the press to write and good pictures for the photographers to take. By his definition he was right about my lack of imagination because it did not stretch to lying awake nights thinking up means to persuade newspapers to print stories and pictures about the president of the United States.

A basic difference in outlook made us incompatible as long as I was press secretary. I regarded public discussion as essential to our government and thought the role of the White House press operation was to assure public access to the president's thoughts and actions. He regarded public discussion as dangerous to the conduct of government and looked for an operation which diverted press attention from disruptive issues and focused on his achievements. Actually, he went a bit further than that. He seemed to take great delight out of newspaper and television coverage growing out of stunts. He thought the greatest thing I did was to stage the children's press conference on the south lawn — a session at which newsmen and women were allowed to bring their boys and girls. It may illustrate the variance in our approaches if I add that I came up with the idea because it was the only way I could get him to hold a badly needed press conference for the discussion of changes in foreign policy. He, of course, liked it because of the pictures that were produced.

The differences had not been a matter of any importance when I worked with him in the Senate. The legislative branch of the government is not as institutionalized in its press relations as the executive branch. Furthermore, in the Senate I was part of his strategic *legislative* operation and he could not withhold facts from me without jeopardizing his strategies. Therefore, when he was Senate majority leader, I could talk to newsmen and women in full confidence that my knowledge was sufficient. The White House was a different story. My *only* job was to keep in touch with the press and I was dependent upon others for my information. He did not like the manner in which I wanted to use it and, therefore, I was cut off. Our relationship became more and more tenuous — especially when I told him privately that I thought Vietnam was going to be a disaster. I had been with him too long to leave explosively and I looked for a graceful exit. It came to me in the form of a medical discovery that what I had considered merely tender feet was a serious condition requiring extensive surgery. I walked out and began a long decompression process of which I hope this book to be the final stage.

8

The Puritan Ethic

An outstanding paradox of the Lyndon B. Johnson character flowed from his entrapment in the rigid chains of Puritan morality. He drank — sometimes to the point of stupefaction; he cussed — often for the sole purpose of shocking his audience; he chased women — although I suspect he regarded them as more decorative than titillating; he was a bully — probably in compensation for his inferiority complex. But in his heart, he thought of these things as sins for which he had to atone. Unfortunately, he had not been born into the Roman Catholic Church where Confession and Good Works could bring absolution. Instead, he was the product of rigorous fundamentalism in which redemption was possible only through self-denial.

Another way of looking at it is to say that he knew of no innocent form of recreation. As Caesar did with Gaul, he divided living into three parts. The only sanctified activity was hard work to achieve clearly defined goals; the only recreation was frenetic activity that made one forget the problems of the day; and the only true happiness was the oblivion he could find in Scotch or in sleep. The concept of reading for the sake of contemplation, of community activity for the sake of sharing joy, of conversation for the sake of human contact was totally foreign to his psyche. He did understand dimly that other people had some interests outside of their direct work but he thought of such interests as weakness and, if they included classical music or drama, mere snobbery practiced by "the Eastern establishment."

I cringed every time he attended a baseball game because he made it so perfectly obvious that he was bored by the whole procedure. He went only when a game was to be attended by a large number of fellow politicians with whom he could transact some business. On such days, I sat at home praying that television cameras would not catch him with his back turned to the field in deep conversation about a tax bill or an upcoming election while a triple play was in process or when a cleanup hitter had just knocked a home run with the bases loaded. The presence of musical groups at White House receptions was not quite so bad, even though it was apparent that he was always more interested in the bust line of the soprano than in the melodic line of the tenor. Music lovers are much more willing than baseball fans to overlook indifference to their ruling passions.

As with everything else about the Johnson personality, this aspect of his life had many complications. The man had a real sense of beauty, which surfaced when he discussed some of the truly lovely scenery around the ranch. He was particularly fond of a bend on the Pedernales River where the sheep would gather in the evening to drink the water. Once, in tones almost reverent, he said to me that their drifting down the shallow bank in the twilight was "like a scene out of biblical times." Occasionally, he would stray to the edge of genuine relaxation or enjoyment but invariably he would recoil like a devout Muslim tempted by an offer of savory ham.

At the end of a whistle-stop election tour of the South during the 1960 presidential campaign, he gave orders to the staff to set up a meal for everyone "at the best restaurant in New Orleans" and to secure hotel accommodations so a thoroughly exhausted group could rest. The meal was a disaster. Halfway through he decided he was in the midst of Sin City. Sharp commands were barked and in minutes a weary, bedraggled entourage found itself loaded onto an airplane (ordered for a pickup the next morning) and flown back to the ranch, where we arrived at 2 A.M. The next morning, assistants were awakened to start another tour.

He developed forms of recreation with which to entertain visitors to the ranch. Generally, they involved the rich resources of game in the hill country which he pursued with a few variations from normal methods of hunting. There was a period, for example, when doves were chased in a Volkswagen bus with sunroofs through which the gunners could take aim and, even more important, a space in the back where a white-coated attendant sitting on an ice chest could dispense shells and replenish drinks — carefully opening a fresh bottle of soda every time LBJ called for another Scotch. Deer, on the other hand, were shot from white or cream-colored Lincolns driven across the open fields like a cutting horse — dodging rocks and chuck holes and equipped with an especially strident horn to disperse bewildered cattle. The watering ponds on his land (called "tanks" in Texas) were stocked with bass and catfish and, for a short space, were surrounded by lawn chairs inhabited by somewhat bemused guests from the East holding a fishing rod in one hand and a highball in the other. It was not very strenuous exercise. The white-coated attendant was again present to bait the hooks, throw the lures into the water and reel in whatever fish were hooked. As the tanks were well stocked, the attendant was kept busy and occasionally was a bit late on delivering a drink.

None of these forms of activity really held any interest for him. He was a superb shot but never learned to load a rifle or a shotgun. The deer that he and his guests killed were never properly dressed (all he really wanted was the rack to mount) and the result was venison tainted by the odor and the taste of musk. Nothing could be done with it except to have it ground into a sausage in which heavy doses of pepper would disguise the unpleasant flavor. He gave away huge amounts of it at Christmas and most of the recipients of his largesse were less than enthusiastic. (It wasn't bad if properly cooked but the secret of the cooking was known only to his own cook.)

The one form of diversion that never paled was a tour of the ranch with extended pauses at sites he regarded as historic in the development of the Johnson family. "Three generations along the banks of the Pedernales," he would muse as he stood in the family cemetery. The next stop would be "the house in which I was born." His mother once protested that he was pointing at the tool shed but that did not stop him from reconstructing the edifice (enlarging it at least four times during the process of reconstruction) and later having it established as a museum. The end of the tour would be the "low water dam" east of the ranch (actually a concrete bridge) and a nearby schoolhouse "where I sat on my teacher's knee while she led the older children through their lessons." Add to these bits of only slightly dubious history a rugged landscape, a few small herds of very fine Whiteface

Herefords and two magnificent — and centuries old — liveoak trees
in front of his house and the tour was a real joy. For his friends and
staff, it became less of a joy after the tenth, fifteenth, or twentieth
repetition.

Occasionally the tour would be extended to Johnson City, where a
cousin, a woman who both taught in the local school and herded
goats, owned some of the original Johnson property. On it was a small
stone house which, according to LBJ, had been the fort that protected
his grandfather (or grand uncle — I could never keep them straight)
when he battled Indians. He loved pointing to the gunports and then
telling a story about one of the women in the family who had escaped
scalping by hiding in a flour barrel while redskins looted the farm
house. It was impressive — so much so that it inspired the late
Stewart Alsop to compose a haunting piece entitled "The Smell of the
Frontier." The composition, incidentally, did not include a description of the heated swimming pool equipped with a floating chair in
which Stew rested, scotch and soda in hand, while discussing the
preparation of the article with me.

I have outlined this at length because it leads to a very important
point. The preceding two paragraphs describe the sum total of
genuine enjoyment in Lyndon Johnson's life. What to anyone else
would have been a charming way to spend one — or possibly two —
evenings was for him the be-all and end-all of nonworking existence.
Actually, it was difficult to spend a whole evening on the exercise
without the trip to Johnson City. The "ranch" was only a sliver of the
land owned by his father, and I am not even certain that it was part of
the original Johnson domain. Nonstop, the whole tour could be made
in less than five minutes, and if it ran a half-hour, the extended time
was due to a visit with Cousin Oriole. His really good cattle were
pastured on other land a considerable distance away where he could
get acreage at a cheaper price than was demanded by his neighbors on
the Pedernales.

In a very important sense, LBJ was a man who had been deprived
of the normal joys of life. He knew how to struggle; he knew how to
outfox political opponents; he knew how to make money; he knew
how to swagger. But he did not know how to live. He had been
programmed for business and for business only and outside of his
programming, he was lost.

It is easy to blame the situation on his father and mother. He was
full of stories which would back such a thesis. He told me once that his

father woke him up at five o'clock every morning shouting: "Get up, Lyndon! Every other boy in town has got a head start on you." Another favorite line of his was advice from his father to "have an objective at all times." His mother never let him forget that he was descended from a preacher who had converted Sam Houston to the Christian faith and had served as second president of Baylor University. Quite clearly, he was expected to live up to his ancestry.

There could be little doubt of the character of his mother. Anyone who knew her — even for a brief period of her life — would spot her immediately as an "achiever" and what is generally termed "overbearing female." But to accept her as the sole source of his monomaniacal striving would be a gross oversimplification. The other members of his immediate family — presumably subject to the same influences — could not be described as achievers in any sense. More likely, he was born with the itch to achieve and remembered everything she said on the subject because it was a philosophy to which he was psychologically predisposed. As for his father, he told so many different stories that it was impossible to draw any clear picture of the man. He once described him as a "rough mountain man" (he meant the hill country of Texas, which would hardly seem like mountains to residents of the Appalachians or the Rockies) and a few minutes later was telling me about his gentleness. On some occasions, he would quote very shrewd, paternal political advice and the next day indicate that his sire had been a mere child taken in by a group of sharpers. It would require a positive act of faith (and a complete suspension of logical thought processes) to take LBJ seriously on this subject.

Had he realized that the whole world was not striving to achieve à la Johnson, there would have been little harm to it other than his personal deprivation. Unfortunately for him, he believed the whole world was following the same path. He could not understand avocations, hobbies, or the loose form of banter which smooths so much of social discourse. When he misread the character of people of his own generation, it was usually because he found meanings in words that had no meaning other than social lubrication. He was totally devoid of small talk. Worse, he had no concept of the social usefulness of small talk.

When he was president, a reporter who had been granted (against my advice) an exclusive interview tried to break the ice with a routine inquiry about life in the White House. "What kind of a chicken-shit question is that to ask the leader of the free world?" he roared.

Another journalist, visiting him at the ranch on an earlier date, pointed to a small liveoak tree and asked whether it was a "mesquite bush." Again, it was an ice-breaking question. In Johnson's lexicon, however, mesquite was something that grew near a house only if the owners were "po' white trash" and the man was immediately banished to outer darkness in his thoughts. He later accused this correspondent for a national magazine — one of the strongest supporters he had in the Senate press gallery — of "telling lies." The statement was made to other newsmen and the result was predictable — the conversion of a loyal friend to an implacable foe.

There was another aspect to this view of the world which also had decidedly negative effects. He was positive that anyone with a profession was interested in pursuing only that profession twenty-four hours a day and seven days a week. Thus, he expected every lawyer to be chasing ambulances, every doctor to be promoting patients, every accountant to be looking for tax cases, and every newspaperman to be looking for a story. Obviously, this belief was based on an underlying truth and had he not run it into the ground, it would have been relatively harmless. But he *did* run it into the ground and the results were not always harmless. For example, the already mentioned decision to abolish the press pool on the president's airplane stemmed from his inability to recognize that the men who formed the pool only wanted a chance to relax. This he could not believe. He insisted they were there to get stories and would write "mean" stories unless they were given something favorable. As it was obviously impossible to think up enough favorable stories to occupy three or four hours of flight time, it made sense to him to abolish the entire institution.

With most other professions, his misreading of human nature was not as counterproductive because his contacts with them were only sporadic. But there were real troubles in his relationships with humanities-oriented members of the academic community because he did not — and could not — understand their goals. They did not *do anything* in the sense of trying cases; making out tax returns; healing sick people; selling commodities; or organizing campaigns. He did know, however, that most of them could write and he concluded that their principal purpose in life was to produce speeches. Historians existed to supply the facts; English professors to supply catchy words; philosophers to give him little homilies (his favorite was: Do unto others as you would have them do unto you) that the audience would

remember. To some extent, his attitude toward philosophy, literature, and the arts resembled that of the proud father who has his
daughter taught to play Chopsticks on the piano and his son to recite
Thanatopsis so they can entertain visitors in the parlor on Sunday.

This lack of comprehension was not due to any lack of intelligence.
The Johnson IQ took a back seat to very few others — perhaps even to
none. His mind was magnificent — fast, penetrating, resourceful.
But he simply *could not see* a concept without an immediate, pragmatic objective. Once the objective was inserted his brain wrapped
itself around the necessary abstractions with a speed and thorough-
ness that was unbelievable unless witnessed at very close range. In
the midst of the debate over the 1957 Civil Rights Act, for example, it
became apparent that passage of the bill hinged upon an incredibly
intricate point of common law — a distinction between civil and
criminal contempt. Very few practicing lawyers had more than a
surface familiarity with the doctrine, as its roots went back several
centuries, and it is doubtful whether it had ever been raised in this
form before. LBJ took some law books home one evening and when
he returned the next day he was capable of arguing the matter before
any court in the land. Former Secretary of State Dean Acheson, who
had an extraordinarily subtle legal mind and who was helping him to
draw up the necessary amendments, later told me that from an
intellectual standpoint this feat was "awe-inspiring."

Nevertheless, he still could not grasp intellectual disciplines that
had no objective other than understanding the world in which we
lived. He desired only the solutions to problems and would listen to
underlying rationales only when he could not avoid them. This led to
some very scratchy relationships with academicians. On one occasion, I thought it would be appropriate for a man mentioned so often
for the presidency (this was while he still served as Senate Democratic leader) to have a relationship with at least some of the intellectuals in his own state. My choice was the late Walter Prescott Webb,
of the University of Texas, former president of the American Society
of Historians. He was a friend of mine, his intellectual credentials
were impeccable, he had a nationwide reputation as *the* authoritative
historian of the American West and he was the earthiest and least
pretentious professor I have ever met.

The meeting between Johnson and Webb skirted the edge of
disaster. The historian emerged from the meeting fuming. "Doesn't
that man know what I do?" he snorted. "He asked me to write a

speech for him on foreign affairs. What do I know about foreign affairs? My specialty is the desert!" Fortunately, Webb's unconquerable sense of humor reasserted itself after a few minutes and he became quite attached to Johnson — even writing some first-rate speeches for him on the economic history of the Southeast and the Southwest. But it was a close call. Webb had a tremendous following in Texas and any open opposition to Johnson by him would have eroded the home base badly. Interestingly enough, Johnson made the same kind of mistake years later when, as president, he met Eric Goldman, another past president of the historians' society. He asked Eric to do a memorandum on presidential public relations. Fortunately, presidents can say almost anything in face-to-face conversation and Eric never appeared to notice the incongruity in the request.

These two examples are typical of a pattern and have much to do with explaining Johnson's problems with the academic community. He never understood what was wrong. He thought he had been very good to the professors and the students and saw no reason why they should be so "ungrateful." It never occurred to him that he was inflicting the deepest of deep wounds upon their souls — displaying complete ignorance of the subject matter upon which some very sensitive men had achieved eminence.

Ultimately, of course, the Vietnamese war became the major split between himself and the educators. He was left with no intellectual support other than an ex-Socialist minority, which favored the war because of their deep hatred of Communists, and a few political types to whom the groves of academe were merely a career stepping stone. This division would have taken place under any circumstances. But I do not believe their judgments would have been so harsh had they felt in him some human warmth — or at least the human curiosity about the rest of the world that is possessed by most mortals.

It may well have been that this outlook toward other people led to one of the strongest of the unfair judgments leveled against Johnson by his contemporaries. It was the feeling that at heart he was nothing but a machine programmed for self-aggrandizement. I do not believe it was shared by blacks or Appalachians or Chicanos or by poor people generally. They could see much of themselves in him — even when he had achieved affluence and ease and made no secret of the fact. But to the middle class, his single-minded concentration on the work in front of him and his interpretations of them as people with the same preoccupation was cold and forbidding. Ultimately, it was the middle class that brought him down — the people with draft-resisting children in college. Perhaps had he understood *them* better and had they understood *him* better, the story would have ended differently.

9

For, Not by, the People

When Lyndon B. Johnson said that he believed in "government for the people" he was as sincere as any man could possibly be. It was to him a genuine article of faith that the purpose of the federal establishment was to promote peace and prosperity for all its citizens. He himself, of course, was going to grab for personal purposes all the good things in life that were floating around. But to his everlasting credit, he wanted everyone else to share in them too. He was not content with making his own pile. He longed for a world in which everybody had at least one grab at the brass ring.

When Lyndon B. Johnson said, however, that he believed in "government *by* the people" the words had to be taken with some skepticism. As far as he was concerned, the popular participation in the governing process was limited to the selection of the nation's leaders. After that, the business of the government was the business of the elected leaders and was to be conducted quietly, calmly, and with a minimum of oratory. He was very fond of Senator Carl Hayden, of Arizona, who was always ready to cut a deal but who wouldn't open his mouth in public except in his home state during an election campaign. "Why can't there be more like Carl Hayden?" he would exclaim angrily. "Can't those damn fools understand that he passed a forty-million-dollar bill through the Senate the other day just by nodding his head?"

He realized that many — if not most — senators would refuse to emulate Carl Hayden and he took this factor into account in his strategy. But it irritated him beyond the point of endurance. He divided the upper chamber between "talkers" and "doers" and there was no doubt as to which he preferred. Interestingly enough, his preferences had nothing to do with political ideology. Earle Clements, on the liberal wing of the Democratic Party, and Herman Talmadge, on the conservative wing, were both favorites even though they opposed him on many different issues. What he disliked were men who searched their consciences Hamlet-like for hours on the floor to no purpose that he could see.

Under certain circumstances he could forgive a speech. He knew that some had to be made for constituent purposes. He realized that debate was essential so votes could be postponed while the leadership worked out the compromises necessary to legislative action. He also understood that the record had to carry some justification for bills, but of this he was very wary. He believed that it was best to secure enactment with the minimum explanation and allow the executive agencies and the courts to work out fine points themselves. One exception to his general dislike of "talkers" was Hubert H. Humphrey, whose capacity to arise and speak *articulately* for hours on end fascinated him. Of course, he frequently used Humphrey to stall off a vote for which he was not quite prepared.

This attitude left no room in the LBJ philosophy for the Senate as a *deliberative* body in which speeches could change the outcome of legislation or as an *educational* body in which speeches were intended to inform the public on the issues of the day. He did not believe that any amount of words could have either effect. In his view, bills were changed by carefully brokered applications of political power and the public was "educated" by the lobbying groups which represented the specific interests involved in the issues. As for "deliberation," he expected this aspect of the process to be handled within the appropriate committees where sticky points could be examined dispassionately behind closed doors.

One of the keys to his success as Senate Democratic leader was his understanding of the strength that reposes in the standing legislative committees. He realized that a hostile committee could "lose" any measure of less than the first importance and could accompany every bill with reports that would insure passage or defeat. He also understood how to make the most out of the momentum that came with a favorable report. To this end, he carefully cultivated not only the committee chairman but the committee staffs. Often clerks found themselves in a closer affinity to LBJ than to the man who was responsible for paying their salaries.

What was never fully understood by contemporary observers of the legislative scene was that the overall Johnson legislative strategy would have gone by the boards had the chamber rung with too much debate. His success rested upon some assumptions that were understood in the proper quarters but which could not be expressed publicly without upsetting a large number of applecarts.

Northerners never realized, for example, how the lure of a possible Johnson presidency softened the resistance of the Southerners to civil rights and liberal economic measures. I will never be certain as to how serious Johnson himself was about his presidential prospects during the Senate period. But there was no question that he understood its value in heading off collisions between the North and the South. The Dixie senators had chafed for decades at the barrier which prevented any one of them from making a practical bid for the presidency. The thought that a man from what had been a Confederate state might "make it" and therefore break the ice for other men below the Mason-Dixon line was a potent force in securing their acquiescence in some most un-Southernlike moves.

The strength of this factor was not at all understood by either the press or the Northern legislators. They thought he was serious about his presidential ambition (which he may have been) and regarded it as faintly ridiculous. What they did not know was that it accounted for some extraordinary pro-public housing votes; for a virtually unanimous Democratic vote against a National Labor Relations Board appointee whose views coincided with Dixie; and for the ultimate triumph of the Civil Rights Bill of 1957, made possible only because Southern senators abandoned a filibuster which could have killed the act.

Obviously, any degree of extended debate would have negated this factor. It would have ripped to shreds some of the very flimsy excuses the Southerners were using to explain their strange votes to their constituents. For example, they once voted against a Republican motion to *decrease* a public housing bill from 850,000 units to 35,000 units. Their explanation to the home folks was that 35,000 units were "just as socialistic as 850,000 units and I'm against socialism." On another occasion they helped scuttle a measure to bring labor unions under tighter control by the federal government on the grounds that the bill contained an FEPC (Fair Employment Practices Act). To put a charitable face on it, both explanations were highly questionable and would not have been very effective had there been searching argument.

The Johnson presidential possibility was not the only strategic consideration. He was also the master of playing both ends (the liberals and the conservatives) against the middle, another art that does not flourish when the objectives are laid on the table. His capacity to exaggerate liberal strength in talking to conservatives and conservative strength in talking to liberals was little short of outrageous. His victory on civil rights was not solely a question of his purported presidential candidacy. Some of the Southerners who did not like him went along because he persuaded them that to kill "this moderate bill" would only pave the way for a "real ball breaker and the next time it will win." At the same time, he was explaining to Northern liberals that "this moderate bill" will break the ice and "before long we will have one with plenty of strength in it." I believe that his true strategy was summed up in his explanation to the liberals and that no other course would have worked. Nevertheless, the morality of it was — and remains — bothersome. Under any circumstances the right and the left will always see and hear hobgoblins and things that go bump in the night. Paranoia is an essential ingredient of the ideologies that anchor the two ends of the political spectrum. The extent to which it should be encouraged is a question of conscience.

As Senate Democratic leader, Johnson was the ideal example of the strength of centrism in American politics. The right protected him against the worst attacks from the left and the left protected him against the worst attacks from the right. One minor example that illustrates the point perfectly involved Senator Spessard L. Holland of Florida, a man whose conservatism was so staunch that McKinley was an anarchist by comparison. Holland once admitted to LBJ that he refrained from attacking him publicly only because "I get so mad when I read the things that Drew Pearson says about you." Pearson, a liberal, muckraking columnist, was carrying on a crusade against Johnson at that point. It hurt and it hurt badly but there were offsetting assets to it, as the Florida senator demonstrated.

Most of the time, it was not necessary to set anything in motion in order to achieve the liberal-conservative stalemate. Liberal Democrats were ready at all times with a civil rights measure to stick on any bill they did not like and Southern Democrats were primed with counterparts in the form of amendments distasteful to organized labor. In this equation, the Senate Republicans played a swing role. They were perfectly happy to join the Southern Democrats in hobbling the unions; but they also had to go along with the Northern Democrats on civil rights efforts. The result was that Johnson invariably could come down the middle, walking a legislative tightrope as could no one else.

What may have had the broadest appeal, however, was a Johnson strategy which enabled the Democrats to win House and Senate seats with ease despite the presence in the White House of one of the most popular Republicans in history. It was a simple but highly effective strategy. It consisted in persuading the public that the Democrats were constantly coming to President Eisenhower's rescue against troglodyte Republican senators who sought to shackle this great and good man. The merit of the strategy was that it rested upon a basic truth — not the whole truth, perhaps, but enough of the truth to be valid. President Eisenhower was an economic conservative and, on domestic legislation, his heart belonged to the moderately right wing of the Republican Party. But his reputation had been built on assuming key military and quasidiplomatic posts in the implementation of foreign policies which had been formed by Democratic presidents. The Senate GOP leadership (first Senator Robert A. Taft and then William F. Knowland) belonged to an earlier generation to whom such policies were anathema. All that Johnson had to do was to keep pushing foreign policy issues to the fore until there was general acceptance of the notion that his chief mission in life was to rescue the general from scheming politicians. It worked and very few people noticed that Eisenhower's requests for domestic programs were emerging from the Senate in a remarkably New Deal-ish form.

The latter development was also part of a considered strategy. The principle was to approach *all* issues by *amending* Eisenhower requests. There were practically no circumstances under which Johnson would countenance a "Democratic" bill. He insisted that the changes be made by striking the language of key portions of an *Eisenhower* bill and inserting Democratic language in its place. There were a number of subtleties to this concept that could not be publicly discussed. Leaving the Eisenhower name on a bill had a placatory effect upon the president, which meant that he was unlikely to intervene in the debate while it was going on in the Senate and unlikely to veto the measure. It also meant that the Senate Democrats were pitted solely against Senate Republicans and, as the Democrats were fighting only for amendments, the picture before the public was that of a Republican president and a Democratic Senate cooperating in the service of the nation while a small group of GOP partisans were trying to throw sand in the gears. It was little wonder that Democratic congressional majorities increased at each election while LBJ was the leader.

Some Democrats were very unhappy with this strategy. In their view, it deprived the public of educational debate which would illuminate the issues and it diminished Democratic chances of recovering the White House — which they regarded as more important than the Congress. There was, in my opinion, merit to this position. But it ran against practical difficulties which could not be overcome. First, Eisenhower had demonstrated his tremendous political power by a number of vetos which could not be overridden. Very early in his administration, it became apparent that a pitched battle with the White House simply could not be won and the legislator who tried it was quite likely to lose his seat. Hara-kiri has never been a popular institution with American politicians and therefore most of them muted their anti-Eisenhower positions. A more potent factor, however, was that the Johnson strategy demonstrably worked. Day after day he was securing the enactment of bills far beyond anything that had been possible during the Truman years. Social Security was liberalized — over Republican objections; health appropriations were doubled, tripled, and quadrupled; public housing legislation became a routine commonplace; public power battles — particularly on atomic energy — ended in Democratic victories. A Democratic Congress and a Republican president basked in the warmth of public esteem while Republican legislators huddled like lost sheep in the cold. It was little wonder that so many of them felt betrayed.

There was another key to the Johnson operation whose importance should not be underestimated. At the center was the legendary Bobby Baker — a young man plagued with a burning desire to succeed. Actually, he did rather well when one takes into account his circumstances. He was persistent, courageous, and energetic. But he was a classic model to illustrate the phrase, "His reach exceeded his grasp." Bobby was intelligent but not as intelligent as he assumed himself to be. He never learned the simple lesson that society has tolerance limits for those who wish to play outside the rules and eventually this brought him down.

Bobby did, however, have a thorough understanding of the psychology of older men who yearn for a son to carry on in their footsteps. He played this role to the hilt and his greatest success was with Lyndon B. Johnson, who, in a remarkably short time, promoted him from a minor supervisory position over the Senate Democratic pages to a prestigious post. Bobby's importance was his talent for gathering information. At this practice, he had absolutely no peers. Part of his ability was due to the fact that no one noticed him unless he forced himself on others' attentions. Among the Senate pages he had the nickname "the mole," which reflected his long nose, his sloping shoulders and his habit of bending slightly forward while he walked. He shared another characteristic of the mole, which was a form of invisibility. As long as he kept his mouth shut, senators would discuss their most intimate affairs before him and it never seemed to occur to them that he would run directly to LBJ with any tidbit of interest.

The amount of information he could glean in a swing around the Senate Office Building was unbelievable. In a brief chat on the Senate floor, he could name all of the sexual pairs, identify all of the hangovers, and describe all of the marital difficulties of the people on the north side of Capitol Hill. Frequently, he knew about forthcoming amendments before the sponsors (invariably, these were instances in which staff members potent with their principals were drawing up proposals they had yet to take to the front office) were aware of them and he always knew who was ready to challenge the Senate Democratic leader. As a result, Johnson had his defenses in place before the firing of the first verbal shot.

Johnson's reliance was not solely on Bobby. As I noted earlier, he maintained a close relationship with key members of the committee staffs. This meant that he had precise knowledge of what was happening to legislation at every step and could, at times, work through friends to reverse committee decisions before they became public. Many senators had a feeling that the committee hearing rooms should be equipped with signs reading: "Big Brother Is Watching You!" They were right.

It should be added, by the way, that Johnson was quite capable of by-passing committee chairmen when they stood in his way. One of the things he did for me was to destroy the myth, riveted into my consciousness in college, of the potency that is possessed by the committee chairmen of the Senate solely by virtue of their chairmanship. Such potency did exist in the House of Representatives, but in the Upper Chamber, committees could be controlled only through ability. For example, the Senate Finance Committee, which handled tax legislation, was chaired by Senator Harry F. Byrd, of Virginia. Even for a conservative, Byrd was too far to the right to be effective. The committee was actually managed by Senators Robert Kerr of Oklahoma, Russell Long of Louisiana, and Eugene Milliken, a Republican from Colorado. When the leadership had business with the committee, Johnson was careful to pay — and have paid — the necessary courtesy calls on Byrd. Then he would settle down with the men who really counted. Another committee was chaired by a man who had become senile. This did not cause the slightest trouble. Courtesy calls were paid upon his administrative assistant and then Johnson would settle down with the man who really had the power (and whose rank was fourth).

All of these factors went into the making of the Johnson legend. However history may judge his presidency it is going to be forced to record him as one of the most successful — if not *the* most successful — of Senate leaders. My own studies have turned up only two other candidates for the title. One was Kearns of Indiana, Wilson's floor leader, and the other was Robinson of Arkansas, who served as floor leader during Roosevelt's first administration. Of course, the title "successful" must be defined. Obviously, part of the definition would be the extent to which the leader actually "controlled" the Senate. But another part would involve the use that was made of the control. Whatever argument may arise later over the LBJ leadership will center on that point. No one can doubt his extraordinary effectiveness in passing bills. But there were those who — even at the height of LBJ's prestigious leadership — insisted there was too much sleight-of-hand.

10

The Time, the Place, the Man

The story of Lyndon B. Johnson's legislative leadership would be incomplete without a look at the period in which it was applied. The tactics outlined in the preceding chapter were extremely effective. But I doubt whether they would be very successful today — and I also doubt that they would have been successful a few years earlier. In a sense, in his legislative career Johnson was the right man in the right place at the right time.

This should not be taken as implying that he was a product of historical accident. What it really means is that he had accurately assessed the social forces of the 1950s and knew what could be done with them. He had also made an accurate assessment of his own talents and knew what he could do. He stepped into the leadership in 1953 with his eyes wide open — one of the few political leaders in the United States who understood what was happening and how to respond.

The year 1952 was an important turning point in American political history. Very few politicians, however, recognized the fact. Republicans read much more into the Eisenhower victory than was actually there. They assumed it meant the establishment of the GOP as a majority party in the United States and they were determined to move in for the kill. Democrats, on the other hand, assumed that the 1952 election was a death knell for liberalism — an analysis that was greeted with cheers in the South and groans in the North, where politicians were digging in for a long winter. As it turned out, the Republicans celebrated their triumph prematurely and the Democrats wrote their own obituary notices too early. Very few of them possessed LBJ's sense of timing, which told him that the greater likelihood was Democratic unity on a scale that had not existed since World War II and the exacerbation of Republican divisions to a point of very severe strain.

When the history of the period is considered, it is not at all surprising that the situation was misread by most politicians. After Harry S. Truman's upset presidential victory in 1948, the wheels of government came to a virtual halt as far as innovative measures were concerned. The Congress was nominally Democratic but the reality was absolute legislative power in the hands of a coalition of Republicans and Southern Democrats. The coalition was far less productive than the Republican-controlled Eightieth Congress, which at least had concurred in Truman's sweeping proposals for the Marshall Plan, Point IV, and NATO. The Eightieth Congress also passed restrictive labor legislation and an amendment to the Constitution limiting presidents to two terms. The Eighty-first Congress, despite large Democratic majorities, refused to undo the Republican laws.

The Truman administration found itself plagued by a series of petty scandals which were investigated just as vigorously by Democrats as by Republicans. The president was a master at creating a public image of chicanery and venality. Personally, he was one of the most rigidly honest men who ever occupied the White House but he insisted on standing by old cronies who looked like caricatures of the boodle boys in the Nast cartoons attacking Tammany Hall. His efforts to defend civil liberties were couched in terms that made him appear to condone Communist espionage. Out of sheer ineptness on his part, the fall to communism of mainland China was perceived to be the result of treacherous activities by American officials whom he had encouraged. The passing of nearly three decades has achieved virtually total vindication for Mr. Truman, and his detractors now look very small. But in 1953, when Dwight D. Eisenhower took over the government, he had plumbed the lower depths of presidential unpopularity.

The final act was Harry Truman's battle with General Douglas

MacArthur over the conduct of the Korean War. The issues involved should have favored Mr. Truman — and would have done so had he possessed a better concept of public relations. MacArthur, who had sensed the public frustration in the United States over a war that was being fought to push the Communists back across a line rather than for victory, proposed a dramatic solution. He sought to push clear through the peninsula of Korea to its boundary at the Yalu River even though the maneuver almost certainly would entail a war with China. Truman turned him down. MacArthur, in a mood of flagrant insubordination, took his proposal to the public. Truman fired MacArthur.

Whether the strategy set forth by MacArthur was right or wrong is a question that now can never be answered. The fact remained, however, that the episode was a classic case of a president asserting the Constitution to control a military leader who was threatening to plunge the nation into a full-scale China war, beside which the Korean conflict would have been peanuts. Mr. Truman was unable to make the case to the public. The general reaction was that an administration which had "lost" China to communism was now preparing to lose more Asian soil the same way. Furthermore, a "war" with China was something of an abstraction, whereas real American blood was being spilled in Korea. The president's opponents, under these circumstances, found it simple to deride claims that a bigger war was a danger.

MacArthur returned to the United States a triumphant hero greeted by crowds in every city while Harry S. Truman found himself virtually besieged in the White House. The mood was dangerous. MacArthur electrified the whole nation with a dramatic speech defending his policies to a joint session of Congress and there were ominous rumbles of the need for him to take over the nation and straighten out its affairs. At that point, the cooler heads of Congress stepped into the picture. The Southerners really were constitutionalists. They were quite happy to paralyze Mr. Truman's economic programs but they were not ready to abrogate civilian control over the military. Two Senate committees — Foreign Relations and Defense — were put together to hold an investigation under the chairmanship of Senator Richard B. Russell of Georgia. Russell, one of the most astute minds that has ever entered the Senate, held *thorough* hearings — so thorough that the public lost interest. The final conclusion was the bestowal upon Russell of virtually unstinting praise for his statesmanship, patriotism, and objectivity. MacArthur retired to a job with a typewriter company and quickly dropped out of public sight.

The aftermath, however, was one of complete impotence for Mr. Truman. The word "shambles" was an understatement in describing the Democratic Party. The more conservative Republicans looked forward with glee to dismantling the structures established by the New Deal. Unfortunately for their plans, they had failed to take into account some details of considerable significance. First, no interpretation could sustain the contention that Mr. Truman's administration had failed because it pursued New Deal policies. The dissatisfaction that led to Democratic defeat in 1952 was based on disgust with petty graft and on a fear that the Democrats had been too naive in dealing with communism. Second, the sweeping Eisenhower victory had not produced similar sweeps in Congress. The Republican majorities were hairline thin. Third, it became plain during the campaign that Mr. Eisenhower and the isolationist Republicans were poles apart — a gap even wider than the one between Northern and Southern Democrats.

The most important miscalculation of all was in the failure of both Republicans and Democrats to forecast the political outcome of an Eisenhower victory. Aside from Lyndon Johnson, few men realized that the election was actually a prelude to Democratic Party reunification as long as Democratic leadership did not mishandle the situation. LBJ was not the man to mishandle the forces at work.

The Southern willingness to coalesce with Republicans under the Truman administration was fostered by the lack of risk involved in the alliance. Southern senators were not particularly interested in the presidency, because they could not aspire to it anyway as long as they were saddled with an obligation to sustain white supremacy in Dixie. Their constituents showed no sign of a desire to lower racial barriers and it looked as though the situation would continue indefinitely. Furthermore, Southern adherence to the Democratic Party had nothing to do with ideology. In the South, the Democratic Party was merely a device to prevent blacks from participating in government (by declaring the party a private club that could exclude anyone the members did not want) and the device was eminently workable as long as the party had no competition. There was virtually no sense of kinship between representatives from rural Mississippi and representatives from the streets of New York.

Many Southern leaders had openly supported Mr. Eisenhower

during the election campaign. They had not realized that his election might, for the first time, open the doors to Republican organization in the South. The times were becoming ripe for such organization. The industrialization of the Gulf Coast of Texas, of Central Georgia, of important areas in Alabama and the two Carolinas had created new classes of Southern citizenry. On the one hand there were blue-collar workers who were no more liberal on racial matters than the legendary redneck farmer but who were interested in protective labor legislation. On the other hand, there was a rising managerial class whose members felt much more comfortable sipping scotch and soda in the Union League Club of Philadelphia than in sipping a mint julep on Colonel Beauregarde's ante-bellum plantation. The Republican Party was much more responsive to the managerial class than to the blue-collar workers. But the latter were capable of exerting considerable pressure upon local Democratic machines to produce candidates who had some consideration for steel workers and textile mill hands.

The realization slowly dawned upon the Southern leaders that they were jeopardizing their controls over Dixie politics by supporting a Republican president. Competition was arising at the local level where they least expected it. They could no longer play games on the national level without fear of reprisal. At the same time, another development took place. Republican enthusiasm for the coalition abated rapidly with a Republican in the White House. The alliance had been formed only because the Republican legislators wanted to block the proposals of *Democratic* presidents. They did not look for anything truly objectionable in the domestic field from Mr. Eisenhower. They were perfectly willing to accept Southern support but they were not willing to give much for it. In short, the Southern legislators lost a good deal of their leverage on the day that a Republican president took the oath of office.

This was bad news indeed, as the Southerners — for all their avowed disdain of federal "paternalism" — were heavily dependent upon federal action to sustain their home areas. They needed dams to control floods and produce electricity; they needed subsidies for their farmers; they needed farm-to-market roads and rural electrification; they needed a Southern bias in the location of military installations which pumped life-giving money into nearby towns. Republican reaction to these projects was something less than enthusiastic — especially when the GOP representatives and senators decided that they really did not need their erstwhile allies.

No one ever made a formal decision on these matters. There were no caucuses, no published reports, no manifestoes, no apologies for past sins. Nevertheless, the Southern legislators were noted for their capacity to face reality and most of them faced it. In self-protection, they were seeking ways to get back into the fold and they understood they would have to pay a price for it. The only question was: "How much?"

At the same time, some long, long thoughts were running through the heads of the Northern legislators. Their constituents were becoming restless. Since the end of World War II, they had been fighting lost causes on the domestic front. They had lost virtually every battle and were no closer to a victory. This situation had been bearable as long as there was a Democratic president in the White House who could send starry-eyed liberal messages to Congress. The messages invariably wound up in wastebaskets but meanwhile they had served to rally the troops. Now the Northern legislators were on their own. They could not continue to hold their seats indefinitely on the basis of alibis for impotence. They had to produce and the more level-headed realized that production was possible only with the help of the Southern Democrats. Obviously, there would be a price and again the question was: "How much?"

Like their Southern counterparts, the Northerners were reticent about their thoughts. None of them dared to drop even a hint of a rapprochement with Dixie. They had conditioned their constituents to look upon any such suggestion as a "deal" to "sell out" the rights of working men and women and minorities. Again, there were no caucuses, no published reports, no manifestoes, and certainly no apologies. But as the Johnson leadership began to produce a few victories, the tone of conversation in Northern offices began to change. For me, the turning point was the day that a top Hubert Humphrey assistant revealed to me his amazement over the discovery that "these Southerners really are constitutionalists. I thought it was phony but I realize now that it was a matter of approach." The ties became closer and more binding and in time the press started to pry around to find out where and when the "deal" had been made.

Actually, there was never a deal. Johnson had realized for many years that the key to the reunification of the Senate Democrats rested in the senators from the Rocky Mountain states. They were in a unique position. They were generally middle-of-the road politicians who had not been involved in the racial crisis that divided the

Democratic Party. In the past they had generally supported the Southerners on the civil rights issues. They did not have to do so because their constituencies did not feel keenly on the subject. They were not tied to rigid pro- or anti-labor positions. Their only "musts" for survival rested in irrigation and reclamation bills and in securing adequate quotas for their sugar-beet producers. These were areas of legislation of considerable importance but which did not draw passionate opposition

All of this had produced a small — but highly skilled — bloc of legislators who were in a swing position. They had flexibility in areas where everyone else had lost freedom of action. No Southerner dared permit passage of any civil rights language — no matter how innocuous. No Northerner dared even breathe the words "civil rights compromise" in his sleep. Only the senators from Arizona, Colorado, Wyoming, Idaho, Montana, and similar states could vote as they pleased. Without them, we would still be fighting for the kind of legislation that was enacted in 1957.

There were no meetings, reports, or manifestoes aimed at the Western bloc either. What did happen was continual meetings between Johnson and individual members. By what amounted to subliminal techniques, Johnson dropped hints of the strength that could accrue to the reclamation-state senators should they act as brokers between North and South. It was never stated that crudely, of course, nor did Johnson ever ask the North or the South to accept the brokerage. It was not necessary. Most members of the Senate who have survived more than one term are extremely sensitive to nuances. They do not need to have the i's dotted or the t's crossed. As Johnson explained the process in a rare burst of candor to me one day:

"Dick Russell and Bob Taft [the Republican leader during the Truman administration] used to run this place with a wink and a nod. I am breaking them up the same way. Give me one more year and the Republican-Southern Democratic coalition will be deader than dead."

There was one other factor to which we have alluded already. No one except Johnson had fully fathomed the depth of the split between the isolationist and the so-called internationalist Republicans. Over the years, the isolationists — or at least those tending to be isolationist — had held control over the congressional Republicans. But the Republican conventions — where Republican nominees had been produced — were safely in the hands of a sophisticated Northeastern group centering around men like Governor Dewey of New York, Nelson Rockefeller, Herbert Brownell, Henry Cabot Lodge, Leverett Saltonstall, and others. Most of them (not Tom Dewey, interestingly enough) were American aristocrats who could trace their heritage back a number of generations and their inherited wealth back to the days when there was no income tax and few restrictions on commerce. These men were sophisticated, suave, and oriented toward international affairs. They had been perfectly comfortable with Roosevelt and Truman in the field of foreign policy despite their conservatism on economic matters. In fact, a number of them had served in diplomatic posts under Democratic administrations. Basically, Eisenhower had been *their* man. He did not *belong* to them but they were responsible for securing this nomination and he was at home with them.

Paradoxically, the defeat of Republican presidential candidates year after year had been something of a boon to the congressional Republicans. It left them as the dominant force in Republican politics *in between conventions* — and there is much more time between than during conventions. The Eisenhower victory put an end to what many had regarded as a happy state. The title "Mr. Republican" no longer belonged to Robert A. Taft, of Ohio — trusted, conservative, and imbued with the innate distrust of the Middlewesterner of his time for maneuvering in the international field. (It would be unfair and incorrect to call Taft an isolationist but he had the allegiance of the isolationists as compared to the Eastern wing of the party.) Instead, the title had passed to Mr. Eisenhower, a man whose entire lifetime had been spent either in military service or in negotiating *for Democratic presidents* with principals of foreign powers. The clash between a Republican president and Republican Congress was inevitable. The man most fully aware of the manner in which deserving Democrats could exploit the clash was Lyndon Baines Johnson.

There was another factor. The times were ripe for action on a number of pressing social issues and LBJ was one of the very few people who understood that point. The years of futile debate on civil rights, Social Security, and housing had led most of his contemporaries to believe that there were no prospects for action in these fields. Actually, many people wanted something done just to get them out of the way.

Dominating the entire political scene was the issue of civil rights. This had become a morbid preoccupation with political leaders both north and south and it was warping the normal legislative processes. To maintain segregation, the senators from the one-time Confederate states were forming alliances which often worked against the economic interests of their constituents and, against their better judgment, the senators from the North were taking stands that accelerated the unnatural Dixie alliance. Everybody wanted to get rid of the issue; nobody knew how.

Johnson knew how. The process will be described fully in a later chapter. But a key was the presence of a Republican in the White House who could send Congress a bill. This eased the blow for Southern senators, as they were not then compelled to direct their hottest fire against a measure sponsored by a fellow Democrat. The next step was to find harsh portions of the bill which could be eliminated. This would make it morally difficult for the Southerners to continue a filibuster, as it deprived them of any claim that the Senate majority was being unreasonable. The final step was — through quiet talks — to persuade the Southerners that passage of the bill would ward off truly repressive legislation and the Northerners that it would pave the way for future action in the field.

Every step worked. It was a legislative triumph. Even more important, it restored sanity to legislative debate. But it rested upon tactics that were designed to fit a special set of circumstances. It is not likely to happen again.

11

A Sense of Timing

The strategic principles described in the previous chapter did not necessarily originate with Lyndon Johnson. He was not innovative in his analytic thinking. His intellectual activity consisted primarily of brain-picking and he lacked the profundity of a Richard B. Russell or the political subtlety of a Sam Rayburn. The ideas he adopted from those and other men, as well as from his staff, became his own so very quickly that it was impossible to trace authorship — especially after they had undergone various transmutations in his constantly churning mind. But one aspect of his political leadership was peculiarly his own; without it he would probably have been just another routine Texas senator. He had the most superbly developed sense of timing in the whole history of American politics.

It was uncanny, how he could predict votes other senators did not even know they were going to cast. He could sense the impact of events upon political individuals and he invariably knew the right time to vote and the right time to decline battle. If politics is war carried on by other means (I have always believed the Clausewitz dictum should be reversed), he was a spiritual descendant of General Nathaniel Greene, the master Revolutionary War tactician who conned British General Cornwallis into wearing down his troops in futile Virginia marches and then trapped the whole British army in Yorktown at a point where the Redcoats were exhausted and continental morale was high. Time after time, both liberal and conservative challenges to the LBJ leadership were weakened by foolhardy charges upon vacated positions and then smashed by totally unexpected flank attacks for which they were not prepared.

Political scientists would be well advised to plunge into a study of the LBJ tactical maneuvers that produced so many triumphs and resulted in the passage of Democratic bill after bill, signed by a Republican president. Many instances — housing, health, atomic energy, minimum wage, education — could be explored and there are still people around who can shed light on what happened. For this book, however, I am going to content myself with a review of the strategic thinking that resulted in his two greatest triumphs — the censure of Joseph R. McCarthy and the enactment of the Civil Rights Act of 1957, the first such measure in eighty-two years. Both were masterpieces. Let us look first at the censure.

To the present generation, the terror that Joe McCarthy inflicted upon liberals and middle-of-the-roaders is literally inconceivable. The power he exercised was a product of a time and a set of circumstances which no longer exist, and if he were to launch his "anti-Communist crusade" today, it would be regarded as faintly amusing and very much out of date. We are much too far from the "cold war" and too sophisticated about communism for the tactics of McCarthyism to make much headway. Having lived through that era myself, I marvel at the reactions of my fellow citizens to our current difficulties with the Soviet Union. These difficulties are now looked upon as a conflict between two competing nations, and no one seems to suspect our government officials of complicity with the Kremlin.

That was not the reality of the late 1940s and the early 1950s. The abrupt change in stance from friendship to enmity by the Soviet Union was bewildering to most Americans. A series of investigations by the Republican-controlled Eightieth Congress had revealed the past presence of a few Communists — or Communist sympathizers — in relatively high positions in the government. It is doubtful whether any of them — even Alger Hiss — had managed to exert a disastrous influence upon American foreign policy. But their mere existence was unsettling to people who had assumed the patriotism of their leaders. The fall of mainland China to communism was even more bewildering, as Chiang Kai-shek, the Nationalist Chinese leader, was an imposing figure who had seemed absolutely stable. Furthermore, his wife, one of the most charming figures in modern history, had skillfully established a bloc of supporters in the United States Senate — the so-called China Lobby — which embraced important elements of the Republican leadership. They set up an immediate clamor for exposure of the "traitors" who had "lost China for us" (as though China were ours to lose).

Unfortunately, the Truman administration misjudged the situation and mishandled it incredibly. President Truman regarded the whole thing as a Republican plot to win elections (the kind of half-truth whose acceptance so often leads men and women into disaster) and tried to blow it out of the water by questioning the motives of the congressional red spy hunters and the China Lobby. The result was to make *him* look partisan (because he was talking politics) and his opponents look statesmanlike (because they were talking about the security of the nation).

To exacerbate the situation, Dean Acheson — Truman's secretary of state — became a centerpiece for the legislative inquiries, so many of which involved the State Department. He was the wrong man to be put on that spot — brilliant, sophisticated, cultured, and exuding an air of snobbery. He was the walking embodiment of the isolationist caricature of a "striped pants, cookie-pushing diplomat" and he understood public communications even less than Mr. Truman. When a federal court convicted Alger Hiss for perjury (for denying that he had been a Communist spy), Mr. Acheson responded that he would not "turn my back on Alger Hiss." What he meant was that he did not intend to kick a man when he was down — a noble sentiment that most Americans would applaud. In print, however, it looked as though he were condoning Communist espionage and subversion. I doubt whether he ever realized the mistake he had made. One of the ironies of the situation could be found in his philosophy of foreign affairs. He was actually one of the hardest "hard-line" anti-Communists that has headed the State Department in the last forty years (I do not even exclude John Foster Dulles in making that ranking). But that did not matter to the isolationists, who realized they had struck pay dirt. They gleefully accused him of being "soft on communism" and his response was invariably akin to his famous line on Hiss.

One of my more vivid memories involves a meeting in Sam Rayburn's office some time in the late forties or early fifties. The phone rang and Rayburn picked it up. He listened, shook his head sadly, and turned to the rest of us to describe Acheson's latest statement: "If that man had just once — just once — run for sheriff of Wise County (a rural area in Texas) where he would have to go out and shake hands and listen to people to get some votes, the whole free world would be more secure," Rayburn said.

Against this background, Joe McCarthy appeared on the national scene. He was a strange figure — basically what would have been described in the neighborhoods where I grew up as a "bully boy." He was a combination of charm and meanness; of quick intelligence and shallow thought; of high sensitivity to mass public reactions and of total insensitivity to the agony of individual human beings. He had the body and the brain of a fully grown man and the psychology of a small boy who does not feel any sorrow whatsoever for the butterflies whose wings he is pulling off. He regarded life as a perpetual athletic contest in which the loser congratulated the winner, and I do not believe he ever understood that he was hurting the victims of his charges. He would often express bewilderment at their antagonism, and I believe the bewilderment was sincere. I can recall an occasion — before I joined the Johnson staff — when I covered a hearing in which he denounced Acheson as being little short of a traitor. After the hearing, I stepped into a Senate elevator with McCarthy to get an answer to a United Press client query. Acheson happened to be in that elevator and McCarthy, with every evidence of delight, stuck out his hand with a booming "Hi, Dean!" He was totally baffled by the coolness of Acheson's response.

McCarthy stumbled into his anti-Communist crusade through a series of accidents which need not be recounted here. It became apparent very soon that he knew absolutely nothing about radical politics and would have been incapable of finding a Communist in Moscow's Red Square during a May Day celebration. His "investigations" consisted entirely of charges backed only by his solemn word that the evidence "existed" (always in some inaccessible spot such as the ultrasecret files of the FBI) to prove his contentions. Actually, he made very few charges but merely named names and left it up to the imagination of his audience to fill in the blanks. It was a very clever technique. Frequently, victims would begin assembling facts to disprove a charge only to discover that he had not made a charge and there was nothing to disprove. This did not ease the harassment that came from his followers. He had also developed to its finest point the technique of the negative. His followers were fond of challenging his detractors with: "Can you name one innocent person attacked by McCarthy?" It was devastating simply because no one can prove innocence — only absence of specific guilt. The real question was: "Can you name one guilty person attacked by McCarthy?" because guilt *is* provable. Unfortunately, those who were bearing the brunt of the anti-McCarthy battle were too demoralized to think of the philosophical base upon which they were standing.

As Johnson moved into increasingly higher positions in the Senate leadership, it became more and more obvious that there were both moral and practical imperatives for facing the McCarthy issue. The only real question was when and how. There was no real danger that McCarthy could take over the United States as a dictator because he himself was not truly a serious politician. The whole thing to him was a game which he played like an overly bright child suddenly turned loose on society with a loaded submachine gun. He never made the slightest effort to build any kind of organization and would not have known what to do with it if he had. He was, however, stirring ugly passions which could be harnessed by better organized demagogues; he was eroding public confidence in the government; he was tearing the Democratic Party to pieces; and he was paralyzing the executive branch of the government, where bureaucrats had learned that the only total security from his attacks was to do nothing. Any positive step on their part might bring them before a Senate committee where they would have no right other than to refute allegations of which they were not fully informed.

The attention devoted to McCarthy by the Johnson strategists became intense as the Texan moved into the Democratic leadership. It was worth taking a cool look at the McCarthy tactics and analyzing them for what was really happening. There were clues which had to be studied carefully and interpreted dispassionately and which merited the study because they revealed areas of vulnerability.

One of the most important factors in the equation was the strange nature of McCarthy's Communists. Those upon whom he spent most of his time usually bore Anglo-Saxon (or at least aristocratic) sounding names such as Acheson or Lattimore. To some extent, this could be attributed to his concentration upon the State Department, which, in those days, was heavily Ivy League. But careful conversations with his followers — who thronged the halls of Congress in support of their paladin — made it clear that this was also one of his strengths. He had an extraordinary appeal to people who had suffered from the lash of ethnic discrimination in the early parts of this century, when an Italian was a "wop," a black was a "jig," dumbswede was one word, a German was a "Krauthead," the word "drunken" was the only modifier for Irishman, and a Pole looking for any job outside a steel mill had to knock the "ski" off his or her name. Joe McCarthy had actually become a spokesman for all the people who had arrived in the United States after the early settlers. They did not care whether he knew anything about Communists. He was making the WASP establishment squirm and they were delighted to get some of their own back.

Another factor of importance was the clear evidence that the counterattacks by liberals strengthened — rather than weakened — McCarthy. He had preconditioned his followers to expect such attacks because they would be "organized" by the master conspirators of the red Communist menace. It was a form of ju-jitsu which was incredibly effective. Mere opposition to McCarthy became a form of treason. It was evidence of complicity in an underground cabal.

Still another interesting feature was the virtual paralysis of the vital center upon which sanity in American politics is based. This had come about because of the unusual circumstances surrounding the ultimate conviction of Alger Hiss for perjury, technically, but for Communist espionage, substantively. When the first charges were broached against Alger Hiss, they seemed incredible. There was enough to the allegations to warrant investigation but the hearings dragged on for months and months before reaching a conclusive finale. McCarthy kept this fact constantly before his audiences. Middle-of-the-roaders were reminded over and over again of how innocent Hiss had looked in the early days and how long it had taken to dig out the evidence. The McCarthy charges were far more flimsy than the early allegations against Hiss but that did not matter. In the minds of most people, two things had been established by the Hiss case — first, that Communists *could* get into the government; second, that they were so subtle it was almost impossible to smoke them out. In other words, the *lack* of evidence, by this twisted reasoning, actually gave a charge credibility. Looking back from the perspective of three decades later, it seems incredible that anyone would succumb to such logic. But they did. In the words of Yeats, the center did not hold!

Logic was totally irrelevant to the problem. What was going on was a battle of symbols in which the so-called Communist spies were merely a convenience. As long as the counterattack was confined to exposes of the essential vacuity of the McCarthy tactics, it was doomed. What had to be found was a symbol stronger than that which McCarthy was brandishing. His ostensible goal was to protect the United States by fighting against Communists and a left-wing that was "soft on communism." What had to be done was to turn the portrait around and demonstrate to the public that he was really fighting the ideals of the United States — a partisan battle for the ultra right wing in American politics. Another way of looking at it was that McCarthy had become the vehicle used by the far right to prove that *it* represented Americanism and the only response had come from the liberal-to-left spectrum.

The obvious strategy was to bring the conservative (rather than the ultraconservative) branch of American politics into the anti-McCarthy struggle. This was not an easy matter. Many Republicans — even Republicans of integrity — had thought at first that McCarthy might serve their cause and had established friendly relations with him. A more serious problem, however, was the disinclination of conservative senators to intervene by expressing approval or disapproval of the *nonlegislative* activities of another senator. For many members of the upper chamber, nonintervention is an article of faith. It is based upon their deep-seated belief that they should not interfere in the choices made by the voters.

A cool assessment, however, made it clear that aligning the conservatives against McCarthy was possible, although difficult. For one thing, the election of Republican President Dwight D. Eisenhower was bound to put something of a damper on the anti-Communist crusade. McCarthy had not developed any loyalties to the Republican Party but he was sufficiently astute to realize that even his most rabid followers were apt to look with some amazement on the spectacle of an attack against a national hero. Even more important was the McCarthy personality itself — something that was very clear to people who looked at him without fear. There was nothing complicated to the man — no subtleties, no hidden goals, no unrevealed ambitions. He was nimble-footed intellectually, he was daring, and he had no more morals than an IBM computer. Above all else, he was shallow. He was not a crafty schemer but a hideous child — a monstrous infant who had risen too rapidly in the world to take a real look at it.

It was easy to talk to Joe McCarthy, who was suprisingly candid when off the record. In such conversations, it became quickly apparent that the man had no understanding of the Senate. He had paid very little attention to the machinery and even less to the men who ran it. What was definitely fatal was his failure to realize the fundamental toughness of the senior members of the establishment. It had never occurred to him that politicians who had survived two or more Senate contests must know something about political warfare. They had said nothing about him and he thought they were keeping silence out of fear. That was a serious misunderstanding — a classic example of the hubris that the Greeks said preceded a disaster.

In the spring of 1954, Johnson confided to a few staff members and a few very close friends that the time was approaching for a solution to the problem. He described McCarthy as a man who had gotten "too big for his britches." Much of his power was due to "walking up back alleys with little boys dressed in Lord Fauntleroy suits." This had been "popular in his neighborhood" and had given him an overly exaggerated idea of his own strength. In LBJ's view, he had grown careless and was certain to slip.

The mistakes came rapidly. He walked into a totally unexpected confrontation with Senator McClellan of Arkansas — conservative, hard-bitten, punctilious about the law, unafraid of McCarthy or anyone else. McCarthy discovered just how tough a man could be and he reacted with fear — fear that showed in his face. Unfortunately for McCarthy, the confrontation with McClellan was transferred to television, where the nation could witness the spectacle of his willingness to bully men who could be bluffed and his obvious reluctance to tangle with the Arkansan. Nothing is more devastating to a politician playing the demagogue's game than a revelation of physical or combative weakness.

The major blunder had really come earlier when, in a casual statement, he attacked Senator Carl Hayden of Arizona. Hayden said nothing in reply and McCarthy almost certainly forgot the episode in a day or two. But it was the blunder of his life. Hayden was the quintessential establishment senator. He controlled all the housekeeping functions of the Senate — the printing, the maintenance, the office assignments, patronage. He was also at the center of the process under which Democrats received their committee assignments. Add to that seniority which had granted him the Rules Committee and a commanding position on the Appropriations Committee and the sum total was a degree of power which was almost inconceivable. To attack Hayden was to attack an institution as well as a man. It is doubtful whether McCarthy realized that, as Hayden hardly ever appeared — except for roll calls — in newspapers outside his native Arizona. He rarely made a speech in Washington, and it came as quite a surprise to me when attending a Hayden Appreciation Dinner in Tucson to discover that he could talk at all. In fact, when he chose to exercise his talent, he was quite a witty and entertaining conversationalist.

The Hayden episode really sealed Joe McCarthy's doom although it did not come until many months later. Johnson began a series of huddles with the conservatives, pleading with them to drop their traditional reluctance to censure a senator for nonlegislative conduct. His argument was simple, but effective. If McCarthy was willing to attack Hayden, he would be willing to attack anyone. If he was willing to attack Hayden, he would be willing to attack the Senate itself. It was one thing for the Senate to withhold disciplinary action on a rogue who was using the body as a haven from which to attack his fellow Americans. That could be termed an argument between the senator and his constituents, who should exercise the discipline themselves. It was another thing, however, to withhold discipline from one who was attacking the Senate itself. The arguments were tremendously effective. They moved senator after senator to the anti-McCarthy camp. In time, the entire political spectrum from conservative (although not ultraconservative) to liberal senators were ready to do battle. Joe McCarthy did not realize it but his most effective shield — the argument that "only left-wingers" opposed him — was removed while he was totally oblivious to what was happening.

The censure motion itself was precipitated by the highly civilized Senator Flanders of Vermont. What followed was foreordained. A committee of three Republicans and three Democrats was established. They consisted of men ranging from the center to a political position several steps to the right of William McKinley. McCarthy found himself confronted with six men who were much more at home with action than with words and who treated him as an ordinary felon hauled before a police court. The censure motion was approved by the Senate on a vote in which Democrats were unanimous and Republicans were divided almost evenly. It was enough. McCarthy had been condemned by the full weight of the American political structure. He could no longer picture himself as a knight jousting against leftism. He began to hit the bottle in quantities almost unbelievable for a man who had been very abstemious when he first came to Washington. He dropped out of sight.

I saw Joe McCarthy a few months before he died. I had been working late and took a secretary home because it was too dangerous for her to walk through the park in the twilight. When we reached her apartment, I got out of my automobile and stood on the sidewalk to be certain that she was safely inside. Another automobile — encrusted with mud — pulled up to the curb in front of me and something black and round and squiggly forced its way out the front door and rolled up to me. "Hi, George," it said. "How you like my new car? I just drove it in from Detroit." It took me about thirty seconds to realize that this was the remnant of Joe McCarthy — unshaven, needing a bath, bloated from too much booze, almost inarticulate.

Shortly thereafter Joe died. It is passing strange that a man who cut such a wide swath in American politics left virtually nothing as a legacy. The word "McCarthyism" is a synonym for unfair political attacks, but I find very few people younger than I who are aware of its origin. No organization survived him nor did any coherent body of theory. Yet, in his lifetime, he had been a major threat to American institutions — a demagogue who could have paved the way for the ascendancy of a "man on horseback." Had he continued unchecked, the consequences could have been disastrous. He was checked in one of the most delicate operations in modern political history. It was Lyndon Johnson at his highest level of skill.

12

Legislative Miracle

In retrospect, the passage of the Civil Rights Act of 1957 still seems like a miracle. It was not truly that, of course. It was actually the close of one era and the inauguration of another. But in the early fifties, the prospect of any legislative action seemed more remote than a landing on the moon. The last measure that referred even indirectly to rights for the former slaves had passed the Congress in 1875. It was a reconstruction act which, like all other reconstruction acts, was swept under the table and forgotten in the rush to withdraw the last vestiges of Northern rule from the South. For eighty-two years, it had been impossible to secure enactment of a bill which even asserted the virtue of civil rights — let alone did anything about them.

For much of that period, no one even made an effort to secure justice — economic or social — for the nation's black population. Most of them lived safely tucked away on plantations in the South where few people saw them and even fewer cared. There was a legal distinction between the status of the Negro before and after the Civil War but it was not observable to the overwhelming majority. Constitutional freedom had not brought with it economic freedom or even a semblance of economic opportunity. Those who moved north to the big cities hoping for a better life found conditions even less tolerable. The result was major race riots — notably in Chicago and Washington, D.C. — which hardened even more the determination of the white majority to hold the "color line." However, the fact that they had moved north did mean they were able to vote and, as time went on, the northern blacks started down the road that had led traditionally to the amalgamation of other minorities into the American polity — ward politics. In their case it did not work. Skin color prevented them from getting lost in a sea of white faces. But a judicious use of the ballot box did succeed in bringing the civil rights issue to the fore. In the twenties, increasingly large blocs in the United States Congress based part of their power upon black votes and this led to the creation of civil rights blocs in both the House and the Senate.

Generally speaking, these blocs were impotent. Their only power was to make noise. But it was an uncomfortable noise that grated upon the ears and, in time, the national conscience reached a point where few representatives outside the former Confederate states dared to profess opposition openly to the civil rights cause. That doesn't mean that non-Southerners were willing to do very much about it. Most of them, in fact, were quite willing to acquiesce in Dixie maneuvers to kill legislation repellent to the Southern bloc. But what was happening during the twenties, the thirties, and the forties was of tremendous significance. North of the Mason-Dixon line and west of Arkansas, white supremacy was ceasing to be respectable and loss of respectability is invariably the first sign of approaching defeat.

On the surface, however, white supremacy did appear invincible. Segregation — de jure in the South, de facto in the North — was universal in the United States for housing, restaurants, theaters, and jobs. In the Congress, it was rare for a civil rights bill even to emerge from a committee, let alone reach the floor for debate. In Dixie, most elections were still won in terms of which candidate could "outnigger" (express stronger antiblack hostility) the other and there were areas of the North in which the practice was not totally unknown. During World War II, when manpower requirements heightened the imperative of using blacks for something other than cleaning toilets, Franklin Delano Roosevelt established a voluntary FEPC (the initials stand for Fair Employment Practices Commission but most people seem to have forgotten the meaning of the letters) because there was absolutely nothing else he could do that would be any stronger. To have granted the group some enforcement powers would have required legislative action and Congress was not willing to insure social justice for minorities even as a war measure. The voluntary group did have some impact in finding jobs for blacks but what was more important was that it kept the issue before the public.

By the mid-fifties, the issue had produced total exhaustion on both sides. Everything had been said that could possibly be said with the only result a hardening of positions and increasing polarization of attitudes. Movement in any direction was impossible because the question was not being treated as a legislative matter. Instead, it was a clash between the mores of two cultures — deep-seated moral beliefs that could not be compromised. Congress is not very good at handling noncompromisable issues. It is a political body whose modus operandi is one of give and take. A determination to take without giving leads to congressional paralysis.

The antagonists in the battle resembled nothing so much as exhausted boxers — pummeling each other aimlessly without the power to land a knockout punch but with the strength left to keep on their feet even when the rounds were endless. There were neurotic manifestations on both sides. The Southern advocates looked at the world through paranoid glasses. What they saw was a Northern conspiracy to fasten upon them all the ills of society. In their eyes, the Northern attitude was sheer hypocrisy, made possible only because "You don't have enough niggers up there to know what you're getting into. If you had as many as we've got, you'd know better than to keep stirring them up all the time. They were perfectly happy until you came along." (Here I am quoting not a white legislator but a white newspaperman whose natural gentleness and cultivated manners would vanish immediately upon mention of civil rights. If his was the voice of the educated South, I leave it to your imagination to picture the reaction of other Southerners.) Frustration had also done peculiar things to the psychology of the Northern civil rights advocates. The feeling of impotence was preying on their mind — a sense that the Southerners had somehow deprived them of their manhood. There was a distinct note of retribution in their voices, and it was apparent that they wanted something more than a civil rights bill that would help the blacks. They wanted a bill that would include every civil rights concept that had been concocted over half a century and they wanted to rub Southern noses in it.

As happens so often in the political world, the polarized atmosphere had actually created some symbiotic relationships. Many of the Southerners were making their political livelihood by "defending" their constituents from "Yankee carpetbaggers" and many Northern representatives were coming back to Congress year after year by denouncing "Dixie fascists." One of the more famous examples involved John Rankin, a fire-eating white supremacist from Mississippi, and Vito Marcantonio, a left-wing activist from New York. Both men were exceptionally fanatical; both were exceptionally able. They were among the tiny handful of representatives who actually understood the House rules and it was fascinating to sit in the gallery and listen to them tie up the entire chamber debating finer points of parliamentary law. According to legend, Marcantonio once approached Rankin and said: "John, I really like you and in your next campaign, I'll go down to your district and make a speech for or against you — whichever will do you the most good." The story is somewhat apocryphal but it is true that when the New York Democratic machine finally got rid of Marcantonio (by a redistricting maneuver) Rankin was defeated in the following election. The two men needed each other.

A few thoughtful Southerners recognized that the situation could not go on forever and that postponement of a solution did nothing but build up the strength of forces that eventually would explode. But these men were prisoners of an unshakeable system. Senator Russell once confided to me that he wished he knew of a bill "that could be passed over my dead body and which would actually make some progress." He added, however, that he did not think that any of the bills before Congress would make progress and that he would have to fight them under any circumstances because he owed such a battle to his constituents.

Lyndon Johnson was less pessimistic. Texas was not Georgia, and while the issue was difficult, it was not quite as unmanageable as in other ex-Confederate areas. More important, however, was his contention that there were areas of vulnerability in the Southern armor. It was fascinating for me, a Yankee who might be able to comprehend, but who could not share, Southern feelings to hear him talk. Most Southerners, he said, were not very concerned about depriving blacks of decent jobs. They had hypnotized themselves into a belief that Negroes were inherently unwilling to accept heavy responsibilities and were much more at ease doing menial tasks which did not require them to make decisions. As for brutality against blacks, most Southerners believed that the age of lynchings had passed (they also told themselves that only "white trash" participated in such actions anyway) and that "law and order" would prevent future outbreaks. As for segregation, Dixie theoreticians had created a whole mythology about people being "happier with their own kind." They thought that segregation was a "law of nature." None of those attitudes were going to change in the near future, in LBJ's estimate, and it was futile to anticipate any "give" on these points. There was one area, however, in which he contended that Southern consciences were hurting. This was in the field of voting rights. Here, he claimed, even the most outspoken of white supremacists had a sense of doing something wrong. They truly respected the Constitution, which was unequivocal on the question of suffrage.

The most important of his judgments was a sense that the Southern Democrats were becoming disenchanted by their coalition with the Republicans. During the administrations of Democratic presidents, the congressional Republicans had been willing to pay a fairly high price for Dixie cooperation. The House and the Senate were, for them, "now or never" bodies. Democratic legislation that was not stopped in the two chambers was certainly not going to be vetoed by a sympathetic president. The Eisenhower election changed things. He was not as conservative as his legislative counterparts but conservative enough to veto anything they regarded as outrageous.

Except for laws to weaken the power of organized labor and opposition to public housing, the Republican legislators were not truly sympathetic to Southern needs. They did not, as a whole, throb to flood control, rural electrification, public power, and parity farm programs that were absolutely essential to states that based their economies on cotton, rice, and tobacco. Furthermore, flirtations with a Republican presidential candidate would eventually lead to flirtations at the local level — thus upsetting the county courthouse machines around which Southern political life revolved.

Beginning in January 1957, these factors gradually evolved into a grand strategy. Basically, it was to hit the Southerners at their weakest point — deprivation of black voting rights — with the strongest weapon in the civil rights arsenal — enforcement of constitutional guarantees for the franchise. Very few Northerners realized the impact this would have upon the Dixie legislators. After all, they *were* constitutionalists, even though they were quite willing to concoct some peculiar interpretations of that document. The amended Constitution — however much they despised the amendments — *did* guarantee blacks the right to vote. The basic charter did not say anything about the right to a job or the right to social equality or even the right to decent treatment by society. On voting, however, it was unequivocal.

Merely passing a voting rights act was not the sum and substance of the strategy. It had to be enacted in such a manner that it would pave the way for future legislative action in the field. That could be done only by making it apparent that the Southern viewpoint was receiving just consideration. In short, during the legislative skirmishing it was essential that Southern senators win any vote in which they had reason on their side. The objective was to pass a bill — but not to ram it down opposition throats. The keystone of the Johnson strategy was to convert civil rights into an issue amenable to legislative solution rather than a cause whose only outlet for expression was to take to the streets.

There was no time in which the Johnson strategists expected any Southerner, other than the Texan himself, to vote for the measure. In the Deep South, that was literally impossible. The objective was to bring the legislation to a point where the Southerners would decide that they had been treated in good faith and would therefore go down fighting against overwhelming odds. The key to that last sentence can be found in the words "go down" and "overwhelming." There was sufficient Southern strength in the Senate to kill the measure by filibuster. Legislative victory for civil rights was possible only if they were persuaded that the cost of successful obstruction would be too high.

In a sense, the Southerners had to learn the wisdom of the Irishman who was the protagonist of one of Abraham Lincoln's favorite stories. According to Abe, he walked into a barroom one day and said: "Let me have a lemonade with a drap of the cray-tur (whiskey) in it unbeknownst to meself." Dixie senators had to let the bill through "unbeknownst to themselves."

The whole strategy hinged upon the kind of civil rights recommendation that Eisenhower would submit to Congress. A measure with no enforcement powers would be worse than useless. The symbolism would be sufficient to touch off an interminable filibuster without opening any space for maneuver. A truly reasonable measure would be little better. Its passage would probably require the sacrifice of something that should not be sacrificed. A truly unreasonable measure would generate so much opposition at the outset that the opportunity for maneuver would not occur. What was needed was a measure that combined both reasonable and unreasonable — or at least what appeared to be unreasonable — sections. To our surprise, that is what we got.

One of the first problems was to convince Northern Democratic liberals that the debate should be on the Eisenhower bill rather than one of their own. What was involved was a subtle bit of Johnsonian strategy. He wanted to fight the battle on a *Republican* measure so Northern and Southern Democrats would not be pitted against each other in a head-on clash. It sugar-coated the agony of the Democratic senators to be able to say to their constituents that the dreaded civil rights act had come to them under GOP sponsorship. The Northerners wanted their own bill because they were looking for "credit" with their constituents. Eventually, they were persuaded that their tactics would divide the Senate majority so decisively that there would be no action at all.

The Eisenhower proposal was so perfectly tailored to the Johnson strategy that I suspected collusion the first time I read it. Of course, the suspicion was ridiculous. A Republican president backed by a Republican Justice Department does not collaborate with a Senate Democratic leader to produce action that will redound ultimately to Democratic Party credit. Nevertheless, it could not have fitted LBJ's purposes better if he had written it himself. No new rights were created by the president's proposal but enforcement of what already existed was lodged in the Federal District Courts with specific injunctive strength to do something about it. At the same time, another section of the bill empowered the federal government to send troops into any state to require that its citizens practice a broad range of generally unspecified "civil rights." To the Southerners, this was a revival of Reconstruction (it became known in the debate as Title III) — precisely the target that was needed.

To add frosting to the cake, the broad powers of Title III were not apparent from the language. Its potency could be revealed only by going back nearly a hundred years for a careful study of reconstruction statutes. For some reason, the cross indexing on this point was faulty and could escape the eye of even a careful researcher. This gave the Southern Democrats additional ammunition. They could (and they did) hint broadly to their constituencies that a *Republican* administration had tried to "put one over" but that Southern senatorial vigilance had uncovered the scheme and brought it to public attention. The true meaning of the section had first been disclosed in a Senate floor speech by Senator Russell of Georgia, which added verisimilitude to the Southern claims.

The Russell speech touched off a heated flurry. As usual, both sides took absolute stands. The Southerners were virtually threatening to revive the Confederacy and the Northerners were insisting that the whole bill was meaningless without Title III. This time, however, the polarized positions did not ring true. It was apparent that the section was doomed. Johnson assembled a coalition of Western State senators, Republican moderates, and those few Northerners who were willing to risk misunderstandings with their civil rights following in order to obtain action. On a motion by Senator Clinton P. Anderson of New Mexico, the provision was stricken from the bill. The Southerners could claim an important "victory." They had "repulsed" an attempt to re-establish reconstruction and that was enough to enable them to survive the later recriminations of their constituencies when they let the final bill pass.

Deletion of Title III was not the only price that had to be paid for the bill. The Southerners had another "do or die" objection. It was a provision in the measure which would permit trial without jury in cases where voting rights had been denied. Here was a real stickler. The Title III provision had not truly commanded the allegiance of the pro-civil rights bloc. They would have preferred its enactment (and, in point of fact, did get it for all practical purposes a few years later) but they did not regard its deletion as fatal. They were not, however, going to permit the law to be nullified by what would have been routine acquittals of white offenders by Southern white juries.

When the full scope of the dilemma first became apparent to me, I thought the world was finally going to get an answer to the old conundrum of what happens when an irresistible force meets an immovable object. There was no apparent "give" on either side. The Southerners were not going to permit the passage of the bill *without* a guarantee of jury trials — and they had the force to prevent passage. The civil rights bloc of senators were not going to permit the passage of a bill *with* a guarantee of jury trials — and they had the force to prevent passage. It appeared as though many months of planning and careful work were going down the drain.

At this point Johnson rose to what I will always regard as his greatest height. It may well have justified his entire career and I know it kept me working for him when time after time I wanted to quit. He was absolutely determined that there would be a bill. He regarded the measure as a true starting point for reconciliation of North and South and he refused to remove it from the floor — despite advice to do so from many of his colleagues. He pleaded and threatened and stormed and cajoled. He prowled the corridors of the Senate grabbing senators and staff members indiscriminately, probing them for some sign of amenability to compromise. He spent hours on the phone in nonstop conversations with the most ingenious legal minds he knew — Corcoran, Rowe, Cohen, Clifford, Fortas, Acheson — pleading with them for something to break the log jam. Virtually single-handed, he kept a large body of very strong-minded and willful men concentrating on a purpose which most of them thought could not be achieved.

Against all reason, Johnson kept insisting that a compromise must exist somewhere. He recognized the justice of the civil rights bloc position; but he also accorded respect to the Southern position that no man should be found guilty unless tried by his peers. Most observers thought that these poles were too far apart to find a middle ground. But using the same set of facts, LBJ insisted that the reality was the other way around — that if two opposing sides had a degree of validity in their contentions, there simply had to be a legitimate way of meeting them both. Every effort, however, turned out to be a false start.

External circumstances made the period even more trying. The Northern liberals did not understand his overall strategy to use the passage of one bill to pave the way for the passage of stronger legislation in the future. They suspected him of seeking to patch up the racial sores in the body politic with a meaningless cosmetic — and this impression could not be refuted publicly without backing the Southerners into a corner where they would have to fight all the way. To exacerbate this situation, the press — which, for technical reasons, is compelled to deal heavily in cliches — described his strategy as "watering down" the legislation to a point of acceptability. The description was correct but the language was pejorative and did not convey the reality. In nonemotional terms, he was seeking a compromise which could pass the Senate — the normal course of the legislative process. The problem was that no one could discuss civil rights in nonemotional terms.

The compromise finally came in the form of an article written by Prof. Carl Auerbach at the University of Minnesota Law School in the magazine *New Leader*. I did not understand it but was struck by the contention that there was a distinction between contempt proceedings as punishment and contempt proceedings to enforce court orders. According to the author, there was ample precedent for coercion under the second heading without a jury. A brilliant lawyer on our staff, Solis Horowitz (now deceased), interpreted it for the rest of us and the key to the whole situation was in our laps. What the complications boiled down to were jury trials without juries.

The last sentence, of course, is an oversimplification. What the doctrine really meant was that judges have broad powers of coercion to compel compliance with judicial orders. Such powers of coercion have nothing to do with findings of guilt or innocence and they cease to exist as soon as the person against whom they are directed decides to obey the court. The line I recall that explained it to me was that a man in jail because he is in contempt of a court order "has the key to his freedom in his own hand."

The roots of the doctrine went back several centuries, and the drafting of a suitable amendment to the civil rights bill required the application of a superior and subtle legal mind. The task was undertaken by Dean Acheson, and he and his staff produced a masterpiece. It was as politically artful as it was legally unassailable. It raised no red flags by statements that there would *not* be jury trials. Instead, it said there would be jury trials for *criminal* contempt proceedings — leaving civil contempt to be enforced in the normal manner *without juries*.

The political implications were profound. Such language gave the Southerners an out. They could go home and say to their constituents: "We beat them Yankee carpetbaggers. They can't brand you a criminal now without a trial before a jury of your fellow citizens." The emotional implications of the phrase "can't brand you a criminal" were so strong that most Southerners were willing to acquiesce in the broad powers of compulsion without juries that were lodged in the courts. There was another implication too and Johnson was quick to make use of it. Should the amendment be adopted, then the Southerners would be under some obligations to the rest of the Senate for having met them halfway. They would have a debt and Southern politicians — even at their worst — are punctilious about paying their political debts.

On the other hand, the wording of the amendment put Northern civil rights leaders on a spot. It was perfectly clear from the beginning that the bill included ample enforcement power, whatever its other shortcomings. A few tried to argue that the amendment "gutted" the bill, but they encountered a brilliant refutation from John Pastore — a senator from Rhode Island who *did* have a civil rights constituency. His arguments — made in a cross floor exchange which actually changed some votes — left the opponents with nothing upon which to base their opposition but a desire to punish the South. They could continue fighting only by claiming that retribution was more important than securing a measure of justice for the nation's black population.

One of the more interesting sidelights of this debate was one I have touched upon already. It was Johnson's complete mastery of an abstract doctrine *once he realized its relevance to passage of the bill*. With it he was able to pull together his coalition and add to it Northern legislators whom he could persuade into the belief that the jury trial amendment not only left the enforcement of the measure intact but was the only conceivable means of securing passage.

Like T. S. Eliot's world, the civil rights battle ended not with a bang but a whimper. The civil rights coalition — an informal group of labor, religious, liberal, and minority leaders — issued a statement expressing regret over the weakness of the bill but conceding there was enough in it to justify passage. The Southern leaders made the necessary speeches for their constituents and when one launched a filibuster, he found himself staring into stony and unsympathetic eyes. One man was not enough to kill the bill and eventually — as predicted months earlier — the Confederates went down before overwhelming force.

The last sentence in the preceding paragraph may lead some to believe that the whole performance was scripted. That is not the case. It was, instead, the production of a master legislative mind at the height of his powers. He had correctly assessed all of the forces at work and had correctly forecast the reactions of the protagonists to the world outside. He had also selected the time to move — and every indication since then is that he was correct. Earlier action would have been impossible; later action meant an intolerable wait for some evidence that the American system was for all of its citizens — not just for the white majority.

This was the point the civil rights leaders failed to understand.

They were right in claiming that it contained only limited substance (however, it should be said that they grossly exaggerated its shortcomings). But they failed to recognize the irrelevancy of the point. The act was a watershed but they were too engrossed in legalisms to see it. A major branch of the American government that had been closed to minority members of the population seeking redress for wrongs was suddenly opened. The civil rights battle could now be fought out legislatively in an arena that previously had provided nothing but a sounding board for speeches. Johnson's predictions turned out to be valid. In less than a decade, a body of civil rights legislation was placed on the statute books to a degree that outstripped anything conceived in 1957.

To say that the legislation has not solved our racial problems is simply to concede a truism — not all problems are solvable by federal action. Even with the best of will, three centuries of injustice and deprivation are not going to vanish in a few years. It does not take any lengthy observation or astute analysis to discover that most blacks are little better off today than they were in the fifties, even though there has been considerable progress for some. I do not believe that is the way to regard Johnson's achievement. What he did was to demonstrate that the democratic system can be made to work regardless of the odds.

I am leaving Johnson's legislative career at this point. This is not a biography nor is it a history. There is ample scope for some serious studies of how a legislative body can be made to work in the record of his eight years as leader. It should be pursued. I, on the other hand, am attempting a personal evaluation and in this chapter I am presenting him at what I believe was his finest. I did not always see him at his finest. But in my hours of greatest self-doubt, I can always go back to the era of McCarthy and the 1957 civil rights debate and decide that working for him was worthwhile. On both occasions, our society needed him desperately and on both occasions he came through. Whatever else may be said in history about him — and much of it will be very unpleasant — that should be recorded.

13

Through the Shadows

If the period of the McCarthy censure and the civil rights bill represented Lyndon B. Johnson at his finest, the period of the vice presidency represented him at his worst. It was a nightmare — a time in which he wallowed in self-pity, emotional binges, and suspicion to the point of paranoia. To cap it all, his customary good judgment had deserted him. Somewhere along the line, he had lost his capacity to discriminate among varying qualities of advice.

The staff members who stayed with him were caught up in a weird cycle of conflicting impulses. To the maximum extent possible, they acted as a buffer between him and the world, and some of them were afraid that if they left, the withdrawal of the buffer would expose to the rest of the country a very peculiar vice president indeed. It would not have been a pleasing sight, but in retrospect, it might have been best to have laid the whole thing bare. The staff loyalty, I now believe, was misplaced. He should not have been babied.

A typical example involved an occasion in which a former staff member — a respected college professor — came to Washington bringing with him the president of his university, who wanted to discuss with officials the possibility of joint projects in outer space. The university president expressed a desire to visit Johnson, who had been appointed chairman of the President's Advisory Committee on Outer Space. I could see nothing wrong with the request. Both the college professor and the university president (who later became a federal judge) were men of excellent reputation. The professor was an ardent Johnson booster who had performed his duties in our office at a level of genuine excellence. The university was one of the finest in the United States and certainly had resources that would be useful to the outer space effort. Johnson's position was purely advisory and he had no authority to let contracts. I called the vice president's office expecting to have the red carpet rolled out.

LBJ responded to the request with a burst of profanity that was extreme even for him. He questioned my judgment, my sanity, and my loyalty for even suggesting a meeting. Why, he demanded, should he see a lobbyist? If he saw the college president, he claimed, he would have no basis for turning down the teamster's union representative the next day and the spokesman for Nevada gambling interests the following afternoon. The two men were in my office and I was helpless to respond without revealing the total irrationality of his position. I hung up and, out of a perverse sense of loyalty, muttered some kind of an excuse. It was accepted gracefully but I could see in the eyes of my visitors the realization that something was out of kilter.

I never fully understood this or other similar episodes. In the back of his mind, it is possible that he believed these visits were inspired by Bobby Kennedy as part of a "plot" to delete the name LBJ from the ticket in 1964. This had become an obsession with him — a conviction that peopled the world with agents of the president's brother all seeking to do him in. Someone — I never found out who — very actively fed this belief and kept him in a perpetual state of anxiety. This reached major proportions with the outbreak of the Billy Sol Estes and the Bobby Baker scandals.

Billy Sol Estes was a west Texas rancher who piled up considerable money by borrowing from banks and using as collateral expensive fertilizer tanks which did not exist. The mortgages on the tanks were discounted and sold to pay off the installments on the original loans and this, in turn, triggered a new wave of borrowings. It was a Ponzi-like scheme which could work only if Billy Sol made a big killing somewhere along the line. Of course, what happened was that the loans pyramided to a point where even a raid on Fort Knox would not have produced sufficient funds to pay them off. The whole scheme blew sky high and every journalist in the United States started to look for the political connections.

The least likely place to look was Lyndon Johnson's backyard. His contacts with Billy Sol had been perfunctory, to say the least. He had received a couple of crates of melons from Billy on Christmas; there was some very desultory correspondence in the files; Cliff Carter, LBJ's Texas political manager, had once talked Billy Sol into a ridiculously small donation to a west Texas station which carried Johnson's Sunday radio programs. The facts were that Billy Sol's political connections leaned toward the labor-liberal faction of the Texas Democratic Party and that faction hated LBJ with a burning intensity, despite the time that the two had been forced into an alliance to oppose Texas Governor Allan Shivers in 1956.

There was absolutely nothing to keep Johnson's name in the Billy Sol Estes story except the LBJ refusal to level with the press. He covered up when there was nothing to cover and thereby created the suspicion that he was involved somehow. His reasoning was simple: The whole thing existed as a Bobby Kennedy plot and to talk about it to the press was to help Bobby Kennedy.

About the same thing happened in the Bobby Baker scandal except that in this instance he was really close to the central figure in the exposé. He had considered Bobby as virtually a son and succeeded in promoting him to be secretary of the Senate Majority at an age when Bobby should still have been in knee britches. Bobby used this — and a similar relationship that he built with Senator Robert Kerr of Oklahoma — to engage in some highly questionable maneuvers involving a Wisconsin savings and loan association, a food vending machine service, and ultimately the construction of a resort hotel on the Atlantic coast of Maryland. Most of these shenanigans took place after Johnson had left the Senate and was no longer Bobby's boss. I never found any evidence that Johnson had any involvement in the deals other than Bobby's dropping of his name to every prospective business partner. There were, however, some things to be explained, such as some rather expensive gifts from Bobby to the Johnsons and a $1,000,000 insurance policy on Johnson's life taken out by Mrs. Johnson's radio and TV station KTBC. There were innocent and true explanations to every incident but, again, Johnson refused to explain. He took the position that he hardly knew Bobby Baker — one of the great whoppers of American political history.

The Bobby Baker story was a dream for any reporter jaded with routine coverage of legislative action. It involved wild women, wild parties, and wild booze. There was a mysterious German beauty who disappeared abruptly when the story broke and later bobbed up in her native town in Germany; there were hints of high jinks in high places among highly placed people; and, above all, there was Bobby himself. He was one of those men who like to look crooked — perhaps because he associated such a demeanor with the word "big shot." I discovered on one occasion when Bobby asked me some very innocent question on the Senate floor that observers in the gallery thought he was conveying to me information about illegal campaign contributions. I reached the point where I would not talk to him unless a third party was present.

Obviously, such a story was going to capture the headlines and hang on to them for a considerable period of time. But Johnson refused to accept the obvious explanation. He insisted that it stayed in the press because of conscious pressure from Bobby Kennedy, who, he claimed, was holding daily briefings with the sole purpose of knifing LBJ in the back. He was so convinced of the existence of these briefings that I made a personal effort to check on them myself. There was not the least bit of evidence that they were taking place or had taken place. I am not a master spy but it is hardly likely that during that period the attorney general of the United States could have engaged in such an organized effort without one of my newspaper friends tipping me off.

This viewpoint did not impress Johnson in the slightest. He merely said I was "naive" and that he would demonstrate the truth to me. The next time the two of us were together with a correspondent, he lectured the man on how wrong it was to ask stooge questions and then said: "I know all about those briefings downtown." It became apparent at once that the correspondent did *not* know about them but that did not stop LBJ. He continued his lectures to other correspondents — a practice that led to some speculation as to his mental stability. Fortunately, the speculation did not appear in print.

These episodes were merely ludicrous. Much more serious was his interpretation of *all* his relations with the administration as involved with "plots." He resisted — to the point of hysteria — the round-the-world trip which later became famous for his discovery of Bashir, the camel driver, in Karachi. He was equally obstinate in opposing the project that sent him to the Middle East for a good-will tour of Lebanon, Iran, Turkey, Cyprus, Greece, and Italy and later to Sweden, Finland, Norway, Denmark, and Iceland. He raved, at least to me, that Bobby Kennedy was trying to set him up.

It was hard for me to understand his attitude. There was no particular reason for trouble in any of these places. In fact, the round-the-world and the Middle Eastern trips turned out to be triumphs. There was nothing about the trips themselves that could be interpreted properly as "setting him up" to be knocked over.

Part of it may be that he failed to comprehend the value of a good-will trip. Outside of Vietnam (where he was entrusted by President Kennedy with a mission to impress upon the government the need for some political reforms), there was no "business" to do and he could not understand why the government would spend all that money to have him make some speeches. Although I did not realize it at the time, this could have been the basis for his conviction that "plotting" was involved. He reasoned that there had to be some motive for every action and he regarded the rationale for his travels as inadequate.

I am led to that conclusion because there was one trip which he undertook without the slightest hesitation even though it exposed him to potential disaster. It was the journey to Berlin when the Russians — after building a wall through the middle of the city — had shut off all ground transportation from the West. This was a direct challenge to the United States, and President Kennedy decided that it was a bluff that had to be called.

The plan was relatively simple. It was to land the vice president of the United States in the city, where he would speak to the people as a visible pledge that the United States would not retreat before the Soviet force. At the same time, an army colonel was to take a regiment over the Soviet-controlled access roads to Berlin. The regiment was to pass through and be reviewed by the vice president on the outskirts of the city. The implications were obvious. If the Soviets were really in a belligerent mood, they could start off World War III with the immediate capture of America's second-highest elected official. No one believed they were ready to go that far. But a miscalculation was obviously a possibility.

Johnson accepted this assignment without a murmur. In a few hours, I and a couple of other staff members found ourselves at Andrews Field waiting for Air Force One to take us to Europe. We were not even certain of the plans although enough was known by then for a few newspapermen to be taken aboard. Johnson, who had been childishly petulant on earlier trips, was serene. He was the only one who slept that night. Even Gen. Lucius Clay, former military commander of Berlin during the allied occupation, was too nervous to rest and it was from him that the rest of us received the full details.

When the plane landed at Bonn for a conference with Chancellor Adenauer, Johnson was fresh and rested — and looked it. There was not much to confer about and the "conference" was somewhat perfunctory. In a few hours, we were landing at the Berlin airport to be met by Mayor Willy Brandt (later chancellor of Germany) and to be entertained at a formal banquet at the Rathaus. The next day, Johnson toured Berlin to one of the most tumultuous receptions he — or any other man — had ever received in that city. To the residents, he was a savior and time after time I could hear people in the crowd chant: "*Gott sei dank! Die Zweite Tier ist hier!*" When he spoke from the steps of the Rathaus at least 380,000 people packed the square to hear him. (This is one of the few times I ever accepted a crowd estimate. The Berlin expert on traffic control told me that careful studies of aerial photographs had revealed that the figure was accurate when the square was packed and it was certainly packed that day.)

Following his speech, we journeyed to the area where LBJ was supposed to review the troops. The staff still had some apprehension, as we did not know what might have happened along the road. We had not been given any clue as to the colonel's instructions should the Soviet or East German guards bar their passage. To this day I do not know (and would rather not know) what they were. But this quickly became an irrelevant consideration. No impediments had been placed in the path of the regiment. It arrived on time and the colonel, after passing in a jeep, joined Johnson and General Clay on the reviewing stand. The gamble was colossal and it worked. The blockade was broken and, once again, normal traffic streamed in from the West.

Obviously this is the kind of experience that any participant would remember simply because of the high drama. But to me there was a significance beyond the theatrics. It was the revelation of an important quirk in Johnson's character. He was a "high risk" man where he could see a relatively clear objective and a reasonable chance to attain it. He was reduced to blithering incoherency by objectives which were beyond his ken. Unfortunately, good will was not within his ken.

Lyndon Johnson's deep misery during this period was notorious. His enemies reveled in his discomfort and gloried in such remarks as "Lyndon who?" During his public appearances he looked like a man in agony and his attitude to President Kennedy was little short of obsequious. For some reason, however, he took to the social whirl — the first time in his Washington career. One of his speech writers was reasonably good at light-hearted quips and the LBJ face began to bob up on the social pages of the *Washington Post* and the *Washington Star* almost as frequently as it had previously been on the news pages. He bought a rather expensive mansion and — using the party-giving talents of Liz Carpenter — turned it into an entertainment center.

It was apparent, however, that the social life was no substitute for active politics. Those of us who had to deal with what few substantive matters characterized the vice presidency found it increasingly difficult to secure decisions from him. The consumption of booze increased as did the number of hours he would spend in bed at home just staring at the ceiling and growling at anyone who came into the room.

Most people who were concerned about him thought that his obvious depression was a function of the vice presidency (described by former Vice President John Nance Garner as "not worth a pitcher of warm spit"). There is no doubt that he found the position disappointing. He entered it with some rather strange illusions (which were quickly smashed) that the post could be converted into a position of power and he swung to the opposite extreme — that it was a post in which he was despised. But I believe that this is an overly simplistic explanation of his inner turmoil. There was some demon within the man himself that would have operated in any position short of the presidency.

I am quite convinced of this point because strange things began to happen during the last two years of his Senate leadership. He lost votes that he should not have lost, he made enemies that he should not have made. He also stepped up his liquor consumption — never slight — and, when in his cups, would rave that he was going to throw everything up, including his family, and go out in the world to become a millionaire. As for the forthcoming presidential election, his expressed attitude was simply "Fuck 'em all! I want no part of it."

The last statement was obviously only half felt at best. He *was* flirting with the idea of a presidential race but only half-flirting. It was a period in which he put on one of the greatest Jekyll-Hyde shows in

history. He would authorize the establishment of a campaign head-
quarters and then refuse to allow it to do anything. He would authorize his staff to draw up campaign proposals and then forbid any
action — even to the extent of contacting potential supporters. He
went on a few trips and he permitted the rest of us to contact a few
people but it was all too late. Other candidates had gotten there first.

A typical incident involved a trip to Wyoming, where Johnson was
a reasonably popular figure. When we landed (I believe it was
Cheyenne) a motorcade was ready to meet us with the press automobile driven by Tino Roncalio, then state chairman. He did not
know me and had no hesitancy about answering newspaper questions. He told us that Jack Kennedy, without any doubt, would carry
the state. When asked why, he replied: "Because nobody has been
out to see us except the Kennedy people. A lot of people in this state
like Johnson but they're already sewed up."

There was considerable speculation in the press as to why the
Johnson campaign was so poorly run. The usual conclusion was that
he "lacked experience in national politics." Nothing could have been
further from the truth. He understood the campaigning process. He
just did not know whether he wanted to run. The result was a
debacle. The only guess I can make as to why is that he really did have
an impulse to throw up his political life, his family, and his position in
the community, and start something else. Something deep was lurk-
ing in his psyche and I don't believe it had anything to do with
"making a million dollars." He was moved by the same impulses that
led Gauguin to desert respectability and head for the South Seas.
Unfortunately, he did not have artistic genius, and the same motives
that made Gauguin look romantic made LBJ look maudlin.
Psychologists talk about the middle-span life crisis. Perhaps something like this was involved and, as was everything else where this
man was concerned, it was colossal.

Whatever may have been eating him, he did arrive at the convention with virtually nothing but a Southern base. The whole performance was dreary. He staged one "debate" with Kennedy in which it
was obvious that neither man was very mad. Johnson's campaign
manager, John Connally, in a desperate effort to salvage something,
made a few disparaging remarks about Kennedy's health. Then there
was a vote and the whole thing ended on the first ballot. The Johnson
campaign had been a sleazy show from the beginning and those of us
who had taken part in it felt a sense of relief that it was over.

Why Jack Kennedy offered Lyndon Johnson the vice presidency and why Lyndon Johnson accepted it, I will never know. Frankly, I doubt whether *anyone* will ever know now that the principal protagonists are dead. My guess is that it represented shrewd political judgment on Kennedy's part. He knew that he was facing an uphill fight and he needed someone who could carry areas beyond his reach. This not only meant the South but the West and, surprisingly to many, the Jewish vote where Johnson had a lot of strength and Kennedy was somewhat weak. This explanation makes much more sense to me than the current Kennedy entourage myth that the office was only offered to LBJ in the expectation that he would turn it down. JFK had more sense than to indulge in a gesture as meaningless as that.

The more difficult question, in my mind, is why did Johnson take the job? His own explanation was that his acceptance represented the only sure method of unifying the party — an explanation that I could credit if I really thought those were his motives. His mood at that time did not appear to be one of unification but rather one of retreat to a different world. It may well be that he was talked into acceptance by Sam Rayburn, who became convinced that there was no other way of defeating the Richard M. Nixon he hated so much. (Nixon was the only man with whom Rayburn would not shake hands. His detestation of "Tricky Dicky" was almost pathological.)

In any case, Johnson did accept and obviously was a key factor in winning the campaign. He handled himself brilliantly in public — especially during the crucial "whistle stop" train tour which was unquestionably responsible for pulling a large chunk of the South back into the Democratic camp. This may have been the only campaign in history where the vice presidential candidate made an observable difference. Behind the scenes, however, the campaign was grinding agony for a staff which felt a duty to the campaign to keep the seamy side from showing. There were some terrible moments — drunken, aimless wanderings through a hotel corridor in Chicago (fortunately blocked off by police) in which he tried to crawl into the bed of a female correspondent (I got the impression as we led him away that he was seeking comfort, not sex); a wild drinking bout in El Paso in which he spent the night cursing and raving at a good friend; continuous torrents of abuse directed at his staff. It was amazing to watch him go out in public and make truly compelling speeches off-the-cuff after such episodes.

The train trip displayed vividly the two faces of Lyndon B. Johnson — one that of a magnificent, inspiring leader; the other that of an insufferable bastard. I can still choke up over the sheer drama of what was essentially a battle for the heart and the soul of the South. And I can still flush with rage over the petty sadism with which he bullied his staff. The people who were traveling with him went to bed every night determined to leave at the first stop in the morning and go home. But their resolve would evaporate to be replaced by pride at the skill with which he battled the prejudices of rural Dixie.

It took guts for him to stand before foot-washing, Southern Baptists, whose ancestors thought of the pope as the "whore of Rome," and tell them to vote for an Irish-Catholic president. But he did it. It took guts for him to plead the case of a ticket committed to civil rights before an audience haunted by fears of "nigger rape." But he did it. Obviously, he did not dwell at length on either topic. His argument was basically that they would live better lives under a Democratic administration and that in order to do so, they had to learn how to give and take with the rest of the nation. He knew how to do it so they would understand. At a little town in Virginia, he boomed out over the loudspeakers: "What has Dick Nixon ever done for Culpepper?" It was a statement that created considerable amusement with the traveling press. But the people of Culpepper understood him perfectly. They knew that by "Dick Nixon" he meant "the Republicans."

Every day, he delivered fifteen to eighteen speeches off-the-cuff as the train swept down the Atlantic Seaboard and over to New Orleans (with a side trip by air in Florida). He never seemed to tire. The theatrics he had devised himself and they were potent. When the train entered the outskirts of a town, a phonograph would start playing, in muted tones, the martial strains of "The Yellow Rose of Texas." As we approached the center, the volume would be turned up to a point where the tune could be heard for blocks away. The record player and the engine would stop simultaneously and a series of local dignitaries (who had boarded at a previous stop) would leave, shaking hands with LBJ as they stepped down from the back platform. He would then launch into a real stump speech (always careful to insert three or four paragraphs which I had written and distributed to the press in advance). It was deeply moving to sense the audience response. This was one of their own — a man who talked their language — and we could feel minds being changed as he spoke. He could reach these people — even with messages that they did not like. There were times when his speech seemed hypnotic and when the whistle blew for the engine (and the phonograph) to start again, men and women would appear to snap out of a trance in which they had received a glorious revelation.

At the end of the day, the members of the staff felt like warriors on a crusade. It was at this point — when he had inspired absolute devotion — that the dark side of Lyndon Johnson would come to the fore. He would lash out unmercifully at his people — touching every raw nerve with a heavy-handed sarcasm that was infuriating because it was so unfair. One of his oldest friends from the days of the New Deal — James Rowe — traveled with us for a while and left behind him a sharply worded letter telling LBJ directly that his conduct was intolerable and that he was ruining a good staff. (Jim also admonished him to "lay off the booze!") A few nights later, Johnson showed me the letter and asked, in a wondering tone, "Who told Jim all these things?"

A number of the staff left him in the aftermath of the election. Most of them had sufficiently good relations with the Kennedy officials to find jobs. (I, myself, had a feeler for a White House job but turned it down out of a sense of loyalty. Where I grew up on the Irish Near North Side of Chicago, there was *no* excuse for leaving the organization. This was probably one of the biggest mistakes in my life as it would have increased my value in Johnson's eyes had he but known.) Those that remained had a fair amount of work to do — with the President's Advisory Council on Outer Space and the Equal Employment Opportunity Commission — but these things did not interest him. He wanted activity — activity along the lines of the Roosevelt White House — and it was rather difficult to launch such activity in Washington where his most important function was entertaining visiting diplomats.

Very early, he discovered the emptiness of the vice presidency. The first rebuff was when he tried to attend the Senate Democratic Caucuses. The answer was "no" — a polite but steely no.

I do not know why he was not prepared for this. From my own observation, supplemented by considerable research, the Senate has always been uneasy with any vice president. He has constitutional functions in connection with the upper chamber — presiding and breaking tie votes. But these functions are so inconsequential that he is not considered "one of ours." As far as senators are concerned, the real importance of the vice president lies in his role as a stand-in for the president. He is regarded as basically part of the executive branch and the fact that he has an office on Capitol Hill merely makes him something short of a spy for a competing branch of government.

Furthermore, the senators take very seriously the concept that each state shall have equal representation in the Senate. Thus, the presence of the vice president at closed-door deliberations is a tilt in the machinery and they don't like it. To them, it meant an extra senator for Texas even though he could not vote. Johnson suddenly found himself a pariah in a branch of the government where he had spent some of the most important years of his entire adult life.

This is one of the factors that make the vice presidency such a miserable job. Generally, he is a man without friends. His constitutional function calls upon him to spend considerable time in the Senate, where he is treated as the possessor of an advanced case of leprosy. But when he heads for the White House and the Executive Office of the president, he finds himself greeted coolly and sometimes not even politely — possibly because he is too strong a reminder of presidential mortality. Alben Barkley may have been the only man who was truly comfortable with the job. But Barkley was past the period of his life when anyone could suspect him of ambition and he spent most of his term as a storyteller amusing appreciative senators over a few highballs in the office of the secretary of the Senate.

One would have thought that Lyndon Johnson's intuitive mastery of the Senate would have told him to avoid the inevitable rebuff. In a sense, however, it flowed naturally from his character. He was a problem solver who never drew general conclusions from the solutions to his problems or from the reasoning that went into the solutions. He was an innovative tactician but not an innovative thinker. He did not care *why* something worked as long as it worked. He understood intimately the relationship between the Senate and the vice president but he could not draw any conclusions from it. It is too bad that someone did not come to him before the start of the legislative session and say: "Lyndon, you know the Senate Democrats will not let you into their caucus. Can you think of some way of persuading them they should welcome you in?" Had the matter been presented to him that way, he might well have succeeded in getting an invitation. Many of his later problems in the White House arose because he surrounded himself with assistants who did not know how to pose issues to him.

The rebuff from the Senate Democrats was matched by a rebuff from the White House and this was one which could have had serious consequences. It represented a blunder on his part — far greater that his misreading of the Senate Democrats, which, after all, came to nothing but a snub. He actually proposed that President Kennedy sign a letter which would virtually turn over the national defense establishment and the exploration of outer space to his vice president. I do not know the exact contents of the message as I saw it only briefly. He did not like opposition and was in a mood where he was bypassing me on projects to which he suspected I might be negative. He was right about this one. I saw it fleetingly through the courtesy of a fellow staff member, but before I could protest, it was on its way to the White House. A couple of obviously inspired stories leaked their way into the press, stressing President Kennedy's bemusement over this effort to divide the powers of the presidency. Fortunately, Jack Kennedy was not really a mean man and the whole thing was lost in charitable silence. I do not believe that Lyndon Johnson ever received a verbal acknowledgment — let alone anything in writing.

Again, he had failed to draw general — and workable — conclusions from problems he had solved in the past. He knew as well as anyone that power in Washington, D.C., consists of horse trading in commodities of political value. Senators and representatives trade in votes; presidents trade in favors, in appropriations, in the distribution of the "goodies" that are a part of national management, and in the fantastic capacity of the White House to enhance egos; bureaucrats trade in contracts, in rulings, and in the manipulation of their agencies to the advantage of their constituencies. Effective trading takes skill — which Lyndon Johnson had in full measure. It also takes a stock of goods and he discovered too late that this is one asset in which vice presidents are lacking. They do what the president assigns them to do and that is that.

In my judgment, President Kennedy was actually rather generous to Lyndon B. Johnson. I saw no signs that he resented LBJ as previous presidents had resented their vice presidents. Perhaps this was because JFK was too young to worry about his mortality. However, he must have been baffled by the LBJ response to many of his overtures — particularly those for overseas trips. I do not know whether he was aware of the antagonism between Lyndon Johnson and his brother Bobby. It is difficult for a president to be certain about some things and on this issue I would suspect that neither antagonist would approach the Oval Office for a frank conversation. Whatever the reality, however, the LBJ paranoia continued to mount. He was convinced that Bobby Kennedy had virtual control over the nation's press and that this control was being used to pave the way for a "dump LBJ" campaign in 1964. This was a period in which he proceeded to "hang around" the outer offices of the White House — something like a precinct captain sitting in the anteroom of a ward leader hoping to be recognized. It was not a very prepossessing sight and certainly not worthy of a man of his stature.

In reality, quite a few things were happening which were to enhance his career. The Equal Employment Opportunity Commission — the creation of a presidential order — brought him into contact with segments of industry and with minority and labor leaders whom he had not met before. They liked him — a factor which became very important when he assumed the presidency itself. He broadened his knowledge of the states and made some political friendships which lasted. Perhaps most important, he became familiar with the Third World — that part of the globe where time had rushed past most of the people.

Had he been a reflective man, it would have been one of the most important periods of his life. He was not a man of thought and, instead, it became for him the period of intense misery. He obviously had not found what he had expected to find in the vice presidency, and while his intellect was keen, it was not of the variety that could grant him inner serenity. What could have been to a philosopher an era of growth was, in his eyes, a time of shame and failure.

14

Apotheosis

My purely subjective impression is that Lyndon B. Johnson was a far better president in the period when he was filling out the Kennedy term than when he occupied the White House in his own right. His performance following the assassination fully justified the use of the overworked word "magnificent." He eased his fellow citizens over the shock of losing their president; he set the wheels of government in motion again; he unified the American people as they have not been unified at any point since Eisenhower stepped down.

Historically, assassination is always followed by the creation of a mythology, and the murder of John F. Kennedy followed the classical pattern. The tendency today is to regard his administration as one in which the American people were marching shoulder-to-shoulder, in the utmost of joy, into a future which would bring humanity to its highest level of happiness. John F. Kennedy himself is depicted as an heroic figure, inspiring his countrymen to battle against the age-old foes of poverty, ignorance, and disease.

It was not really like that. Kennedy was a president who was elected by a hairline plurality (not even a majority) and who had not succeeded in mobilizing public sentiment behind his programs. He demonstrated high courage in accepting full responsibility for the debacle of the Bay of Pigs and in his steadiness during the Cuban missile crisis. He was an appealing figure — young, vigorous, a fitting representative of the American generation that defeated Hitler, Mussolini, and Tojo. But he was not a unifying leader. He simply did not know how to bring people together.

There were a number of reasons for this situation. The most important was that during his occupancy the White House took on the appearance of a sanctuary for Boston Irish ward healers and Eastern establishment intellectuals. There was too much Harvard and Honey John Fitzgerald and not enough Tulane and Mister Crump. The parties were too sophisticated and the men and women too well dressed. And above all, there was simply too much youth — too much touch football on the beaches, too many stories about people falling into swimming pools, too many inneundoes about Hollywood stars. Had the Kennedys been a hereditary monarchy, such things might have brightened up pale and lusterless lives. But they were not of royal blood and a tone of resentment became evident in the mail we were receiving in the vice president's office.

It was during this period that I became aware of the crucial importance of the symbolism inherent in the White House. It is fashionable at this time to deplore "symbolism" and "the public image." But regardless of what *should* exist in the state of Utopia, the political process in the United States turns upon them and they are not to be disregarded. The Kennedy administration had not comprehended these elementary forces in American politics and, by ignoring them, succeeded in looking sectional.

The Kennedy trip to Texas was actually undertaken because things were falling apart in that crucial state. In those days, the legendary Texas oil millionaires had a custom of bankrolling *both* political parties (their hearts were with the Republicans but they always took out some insurance by giving to the other side) and to lose that source of financing would have been a serious blow. It was really not a good time for the president to make an appearance in the state and he did so against Johnson's advice and without asking the help of either Johnson or his staff. The result was a political disaster which no one noticed simply because of the greater disaster of the assassination. No wounds were healed and the arrangements were so badly mishandled that they increased — rather than decreased — tensions.

I doubt whether any man ever received such a tremendous grant of power with so much grace as did Lyndon B. Johnson. The situation brought out the finest that was in him. Almost at once, the whining, self-pitying caricature of Throttlebottom vanished and he became the LBJ of the McCarthy censure and the passage of the 1957 Civil Rights Act. By the time his plane touched down at Andrews Air Force Base on the return from Dallas, he had set upon his goal and devised strategies to reach it. He understood the nationwide shock over the assassination and realized he had to reassure Americans that their government was strong and lasting. He would build the reassurance by keeping as many of the Kennedy people in government as would stay and by pushing through Congress the Kennedy legislative program which had been stalled on dead center.

During this whole period, there was no trace of the ugly arrogance which had made him so disliked in many quarters. He drove his staff mercilessly; but it was a staff that understood the high stakes and was ready to be driven. He remained subject to unexpected outbursts of temper and to occasional wild rages. But they passed as rapidly as they came. It seemed to me that there was too much action simply for the sake of action. But I could not really argue since he was getting results. The Kennedy program *did* go through Congress. International crises *were* being solved. Unfortunately, no one who had the LBJ ear really noticed Vietnam or realized that it would become a devouring monster which would finally engulf a half-million American casualties — including LBJ himself.

The transitional performance was so successful that by the time the 1964 campaign season rolled around, the whole thing was cut and dried. It was doubtful whether anyone could defeat him and the abler Republican candidates retired to the sidelines. There were murmurs of a possible challenge to him at the Democratic National Convention from Bobby Kennedy but no one took the challenge very seriously. It would have been suicidal.

Johnson campaigned as though there were a real contest with the outcome in doubt. In time I came to understand that the *act* of campaigning had an importance to him that was totally unrelated to the goals. There was some form of vitalizing force in frenzied crowds that drove him into a state of ecstasy. He loved working his way down a line of people, using both hands so he could touch two at a time. The famed LBJ handshake was not truly a clasp of palms but a tap delivered on the back of the outstretched hands. Invariably, the image that leaped into my mind was that of a medieval monarch touching peasants for scrofula.

What was even more interesting was the scene that invariably followed a session with a crowd. Despite his tapping technique, some people would always be able to grasp his palm for a fleeting moment. In such instances, it would be necessary for him to tear loose — leaving long scratches on the back of his hand. He loved those scratches. A medical attendant aboard Air Force One was ready with some soothing ointment for a gentle massage. LBJ would insist that everyone on the plane cluster around during the massage period and he would point lovingly to each scratch, describing in detail the person responsible for it. The first time I witnessed the performance, it seemed to me that he was thinking in terms of the Stigmata from the Cross. But the performance was much too sensual for such an interpretation. There was something post-orgasmic about the scene. A psychiatrist could have had a field day.

It is doubtful whether the size of his victory — unparalleled in terms of popular vote — was due to his campaigning. More likely, it was a combination of gratitude for his splendid conduct when he took over the presidency and of Goldwater's proclivity for frightening the devil out of people. Whatever the reason, however, it seems to me that there is little doubt about the effect. His presidential style changed overnight and it was not a good change. In the United States, the election process contains within itself some elements of sanctification and I believe that he advanced that concept to one of deification. He knew that he had "arrived" and he was going to make the most of it. In one of our increasing squabbles over how the Press Office of the White House was to be run, he said to me: "I've been kissing asses all my life and I don't have to kiss them anymore. Tell those press bastards of yours that I'll see them when I want to and not before." (I had been urging him to hold a long overdue press conference.)

As far as the press was concerned, not "kissing asses" meant the virtual destruction of traditional customs for dealing with journalists. The press pools were abolished aboard Air Force One; the institution of "the lid" (assurance that nothing newsworthy would be released for a brief time period) was abandoned; travel schedules were deliberately withheld. None of these things seemed like "ass kissing" to me. On the contrary, they were businesslike ways of dealing with journalists which had grown out of necessity. The press pools were instituted by former Press Secretary Jim Haggerty when President Eisenhower's airplane made an unscheduled landing in Tennessee one evening and local reporters — unfamiliar with White House customs — wrote some unfortunate stories. The "lid" gave newsmen and newswomen an opportunity to leave the White House and get some lunch. Travel schedules gave people some opportunity to plan their lives. It reached a point where no one connected with the White House could schedule any weekend relaxation because an unexpected trip to Texas might materialize.

On all these matters, I am not certain whether he was being obtuse or taking a sadistic delight in tormenting the press. Travel was a simple matter for him. He could decide at 3 P.M. that he wanted to spend an evening on the ranch and all he had to do was tell an aide. Within twenty minutes, a helicopter would set down on the south lawn to whisk him to Andrews Field, where a luxurious 707 was waiting to take him either to San Antonio or Austin, where another helicopter was ready to take him to the ranch. He did not even have to pack a bag. That chore was handled by an Air Force sergeant who kept suitcases ready at all times. He thought — or pretended to think — that the White House press corps could move as easily as he did. That was one argument I could not win.

I did win a few. He tried to abolish the daily press briefings by the press secretary but drew back when I threatened to resign. He tried to abolish the custom of chartering commercial airplanes for the press (so there will be no misunderstanding, the press pays for the airplanes even though the White House arranges the charter). His obvious thought was to make them dependent upon government aircraft he could control. Fortunately, none were suitable and he had to abandon that project. But it didn't matter whether I won or lost. The only way to curry favor with him in this period was to damn the press. Some White House assistants became quite expert at convincing him that they were fighting his battle against "those newspaper bastards" and then explaining (off-the-record, of course) to reporters how they were battling to open up sources of information for them. These were the assistants that arose the highest in his esteem. I never got over my amazement at his gullibility or the gullibility of those members of the Fourth Estate who fell for the act. It should be added that a few of them were playing the same game. The surest route to an exclusive set of pictures by the White House photographer or an advance peek at presidential plans was to get him alone (difficult but not impossible) and sympathize with him over his treatment by the others.

What happened to the press during this period is not itself important. Journalists have been dealing with hostile government officials for more than two and one-half centuries. They have developed many techniques for getting the news, and in the United States, where the right to print is guaranteed by the Constitution, a president cannot hide anything of importance for a significant period of time. Furthermore, there is little point in a president currying favor with the press. The American journalist has many faults but the tradition of printing news when it happens is deeply ingrained. No one is going to talk a reporter out of carrying a bad story because he or she has been the recipient of a favor. Similarly, if a real story is good, a journalist is going to write and print it even though he or she has been given the short end of the stick. It is possible to secure "puff pieces" by judicious wining and dining and to provoke "hatchet" pieces by being nasty but I have never seen an example of either one that really helped or hurt a politician.

There is another side to the coin, however. It is that the manner in which a president treats the press eventually becomes the manner in which he treats the public. Journalists, after all, are a part of the public — the only part that the president sees every day. Their reactions are similar to those of their fellow Americans, even though they will have them somewhat sooner because they are closer to the seat of power. A man who is no longer dealing with reporters in a civilized way will soon find himself dealing with others along the same lines. That is what happened to Lyndon B. Johnson. His battle with the press became a large-scale battle with important segments of the public.

In the election, he had lost what had been his greatest political asset — his extraordinary sensitivity to what people were thinking and how they were responding. Very early in his administration, it became apparent that something was wrong. I found myself especially disturbed by what historically was a very minor incident but an incident that was totally out of keeping with his political acumen. It was his strange behavior over the selection of a representative to attend the funeral of Winston Churchill.

In the normal course of events, he should have attended the funeral himself. Churchill, after all, was a colossal figure — a man who could not be ignored by history. Johnson, however, was suffering from an attack of flu and it was generally recognized that the inclement British weather could be disastrous. It was expected that he would appoint the newly elected Vice President Hubert Humphrey to take his place. He did not. In fact, he refused to even discuss the matter with me or with officials of the State Department. The questions at my daily press briefings became more and more insistent — especially from the British correspondents. It was obvious that a major scandal was brewing and that an important ally had a sense of affront. At the very last minute, when the British press and the British government were getting ready for some open expostulations, he appointed Chief Justice Earl Warren to go to the funeral. This immediately raised the question of a slight to Humphrey. Johnson ducked this one by explaining that Warren was the head of a "coordinate branch of the government" and therefore outranked the vice president. The explanation fooled no one but it was adequate for a face saver.

During this entire period, his treatment of Humphrey was very bad. It may have been that he felt keenly the indignities that he believed had been visited on him as vice president and he wanted to take them out on someone else. An alternative explanation might be that Humphrey's presence made him think too much of his own mortality — a point upon which he had been very sensitive since his heart attack in 1955. But whatever it was, he took extraordinary steps to keep Humphrey in the dark. The vice president received what little information about the White House that came his way by calling me daily. He had been a close friend of mine for many years and I refused to drop the friendship because of LBJ. The other White House assistants did not feel the same way. Unfortunately, I could not be too helpful, as the president had begun to cut me off from sources of information. He was afraid that whatever I knew, I might give to the press.

Again, my problems and the vice president's problems were not of earth-shaking importance. The press secretary is merely a spokesman for the president, and the vice president, at best, is an understudy. What was important about the whole episode was what it revealed about his attitude toward people. He felt he "had it made" and was in the state of bliss where he no longer had to worry about people and the political skills that had brought him to the White House.

There were other indications — again, of no great importance — of this attitude. One of the most marked changes was his easy acceptance of presidential perquisites he had forsworn before the election.

One of his early decisions when he entered the White House after the Kennedy assassination was to do away with Camp David and the presidential yachts on the Potomac. He believed that these were bad

symbols which could turn the American people against the presidency. I never agreed with him on that point. Personally, I doubt
whether Americans begrudge the president of the United States a
few luxuries that are readily available to the heads of almost any
medium-sized corporation. The cost is relatively small and the benefits in terms of presidential health are tremendous. Johnson did not
agree with this viewpoint and I made no effort to argue with him. It
seemed to me in 1964 that there was no point in disputing him on the
question of public opinion.

I was quite startled to discover sometime after the election that
Camp David was open and the presidential yachts had been put back
into service. I had absolutely no objections (not that it would have
made the slightest difference if I had) but the change in attitude was
startling. I had been left with the impression that the camp had been
fully decommissioned and the yachts sold. I sometimes wonder
whether this "impression" was something he deliberately created.
Whatever may have happened, however, he had no reluctance to use
the facilities which meant glorious weekends in the mountains and
pleasant cruises down the Potomac in the evening. On these cruises,
I could not avoid asking myself a question, however. If his original
reluctance had been due to a desire to avoid bad public reactions, *was
his present enjoyment traceable to a feeling that public reaction no
longer counted?*

As time went on, the evidence of indifference began to pile higher
and higher. He became increasingly cavalier in his treatment of both
organizations and individuals. He and I had come to a parting of the
ways in the summer of 1965 (although I stayed in the White House for
another year to recover from my foot surgery) and the burden of
dealing with the public fell on other shoulders. It was during this
period that most of the stories about his boorishness originated —
showing a belly scar to the public; snatching food off the plate of a
diplomat's wife at a luncheon; telling his subordinates that he wanted
a "kiss-my-ass-at-high-noon-in-Macy's-window loyalty." Perhaps the
climax came in 1966 when he led Democrats all over the United
States to believe he would campaign for them only to cancel out at the
last minute on a very flimsy excuse.

I believe this attitude had a direct relationship to the debacle of
Vietnam. He did not, in my judgment, correctly gauge the depth of
opposition to the war, and this was unlike him. One of his strengths
had always been a recognition of the necessity for public acquies-

cence, however reluctant, in any government program. He did not believe that intellectual merit by itself was sufficient to make anything work. When he used the phrase "government by consent of the governed" he really meant it — although he was not above a bit of hoodwinking to gain that consent. He remembered Prohibition and the futile attempts to enforce a law that the people did not really want.

The fact is that he stayed with Vietnam when all of his senses should have told him that it was a losing proposition. I can explain this only in terms of the corrupting influence of the White House. There people fade and government rests upon equations that balance perfectly in the computer but somehow become skewed in society.

I cannot help the feeling that the whole nation would have been spared a major tragedy had he been able to carry on as an "interim" president without the sanctification of winning an election. Lyndon B. Johnson was ideally adapted for the parliamentary system, where no battles are ever won finally or lost finally. His talents fitted him to the rough and tumble of daily debate and of staunch opposition. He was a superb battlefield commander but a poor strategist. He needed opposition — personal, face-to-face opposition — and that is the one thing that the White House does not provide.

The accepted wisdom of our times ascribes Lyndon Johnson's downfall to Vietnam. This, I believe to be an oversimplification. Had it not been for Vietnam, something else would have brought his career to an end. It was not the issue but his approach to the issue.

15

Vietnam

There is a cosmic irony in the role played by Vietnam in Lyndon Johnson's career. There was nothing he wanted less than to be a "war president." This was readily apparent in the epitaphs he constantly composed for himself. He hoped that by suitable public relations, he could persuade posterity to attach to his name what he regarded as "good" adjectives. He would, on occasion, sit up late into the night with staff members looking for the precise language. His favorite was "the education president" but he had others which were a close second. Generally, they involved public health, public power, or the abolition of poverty.

What increased the irony was the fact that Vietnam turned against him that group in society whose approbation he most desired — the college students. Nothing bewildered him more than the sieges of the White House by half-naked hippies chanting: "Hey! Hey! LBJ! How many kids have you killed today?" He thought he had done everything for them — college loans, scholarships, subsidies — and he considered their conduct nothing but the grossest ingratitude. They were not showing the same concern for his problem that he had shown for their problems — or, at least, that was the way he reasoned.

At the time he entered the White House it would have been relatively simple to disengage from Vietnam. Only a few thousands of American troops were in that country and all of them were professional soldiers. Those who were there were instructors and even though a few of them had engaged in some fighting, they had not done so as a unit. Furthermore, this war had made very little impression upon the American people. The populace as a whole hardly knew of the existence of the country let alone the complicated nature of the issues that were in dispute. Actually, until the flare-up in the Tonkin Gulf, Vietnam did not loom very large in White House thinking. Other issues were on the front burner.

Johnson, himself, was skeptical of the whole enterprise. He had memories of the debates over whether the United States should intervene to rescue the French at Dien Bien Phu. Those debates had impressed upon him the classic American military doctrine which was opposed to fighting a land war in Asia. Why did he not pull out when the pulling was good?

One possible answer may lie in a simple misunderstanding. I vividly remember the first meeting he called in the White House after the assassination of President Kennedy. Present were the members of the Cabinet, Adlai Stevenson (ambassador to the United Nations), and the top Johnson and Kennedy staff people. The atmosphere in the room was both strained and strange. It took me some time to realize what was wrong. The Kennedy people knew the realities of power and they were looking to him for a cue to their future conduct. *He, on the other hand, was looking to them for a cue as to what Kennedy would have done.* His lifetime in politics had taught him that what counted was the opinion *of the man who had been elected*. He did not want to take off on his own until he had been elected.

It occurred to me that day that this was a situation that could lead to mischief. It is rather difficult to play "follow the leader" when the leader thinks he should be a follower. Misunderstandings can arise easily. He made it clear that he wanted them all to stay and most of them did. He worked with them for several months before he began branching off on his own. During those months, it would have been entirely possible for him to interpret the Kennedy staffers as believing that JFK would have *pressed* the war in Vietnam and for the Kennedy staffers to interpret LBJ as *wanting* to press the war in Vietnam. Some of the Kennedy staffers said later that JFK intended to pull out of Vietnam after the 1964 election but I do not believe they really know. I do not think this is dishonesty on their part — just the kind of self-deceit of which every human is capable. They did not make this remarkable discovery until *after* Vietnam became unpopular.

Whatever may have started the involvement, it is not too difficult to trace its continuation. Primarily, it was a "nickel-and-dime" affair plus a psychology in which small commitments led to other and larger commitments. A handful of "instructors" led to larger increments of fighting men, who, in turn, started to engage in fire fights which in turn led commanders on the scene to demand more troops to protect those who were already there, and so forth and so on until half a million soldiers were deployed.

Even more important was the impact upon Lyndon Johnson of every American casualty. He felt a deep responsibility for the wounded and the dead and he translated this into a determination that their suffering should not be in vain. To him, this meant that the United States had to "win" in order to vindicate its casualties and that to abandon the battlefield was to turn American backs on the sacrifice of our soldiers. Unfortunately, he did not reflect very much on the meaning of the word "win" nor did he probe the young people who were being drafted to bring about the "vindication." Somewhere along the line, he had picked up the idea that they must feel as he did.

There were some other forces at work which reinforced his determination. As vice president, he had visited Vietnam and made some extravagant promises (or, at least, had used extravagant language to make promises) of United States support against North Vietnam. He felt that this had left him with something of an obligation. In addition, he had strong memories of the era in which the Republican Party tore the Democratic Party to shreds on the issue of the fall of mainland China to the Communists. He believed that another Communist victory on the mainland of Asia could open up another "era of McCarthyism."

The most important factor, however, was the American government itself. Once he had clearly committed himself, the entire apparatus of the Defense Department, the State Department, the CIA, and the USIA was dedicated to making his commitment work.

To me, this was one of the most important revelations of my tour in the White House. A presidential decision forecloses further debate at the levels of government where it is most needed. To be sure, a few individuals may still dissent (perhaps, like George Ball, even to the president himself) but this is nothing compared to the huge bureaucracy which is grinding out the facts and the figures to back the chief executive's stand. It is not a process of dishonesty. It is a simple question of the behavior of facts once a decision has been made. It is true in any walk of life that data will arrange themselves to fit preconceived conclusions. Otherwise, why should every Ph.D. thesis prove the point the author set out to test?

The few dissenters who could reach him made absolutely no impression. I can recall one occasion where — during a National Security Council meeting — it seemed to me that the Defense Department experts were somewhat imaginative in their estimates of Viet Cong casualties. I wrote out a probing question and passed it to him surreptitiously — a common practice over the years I had worked for him. He looked at it, ostentatiously tore it up, and gave me the kind of look that meant I should never do anything like that again. My skepticism of the whole venture was growing rapidly at this time and it was quite a jolt to discover that, as far as I was concerned, it was a subject off limits.

His attitude, at first, puzzled me greatly. He, himself, was predicting the doom of his presidency in Vietnam. With a few drinks under his belt, he was ready to tell anyone within hearing range that the war would be his downfall. Fortunately, there were some controls over who could get within hearing range while he was president and, as a rule, the people who heard him were the kind who could keep their mouths shut. I did have one bad night at Camp David when he entertained a small group of very eminent correspondents and really spilled his heart out to them. They all got so soused that night, however, that their memories of some startling revelations were lost in colossal hangovers.

It was not until this incident that I realized what was really bothering him. He felt he had an obligation to continue the war but he also felt he was not going to win it. In his view, he could go down in history as "the first president ever to lose a war." It was bad history and even worse reasoning but it explains many things. Above all, it explained to me why he was not interested in anyone like me who was developing strong feelings that the United States should just pull out because it had no business in Vietnam in the first place.

At times, he would deceive himself by comparing Vietnam to the situation in Greece that followed World War II. Obviously, he was hoping to be regarded as a man who had emulated Harry S. Truman and stood up against communism when it was crucial. This was one he was unable to sell, however, even to his strongest supporters. The differences between Greece — not only a Western country but the cradle of Western civilization — and Vietnam — a Buddhist enclave — were too striking for the comparison to withstand much inspection. Furthermore, there was no Tito handy to seal off the refugee havens for Viet Cong troops — a crucial factor in the suppression of the Greek Communist revolutionaries.

He had always been fond of the old frontier story about the man who had a bear by the tail and could not let go. That was precisely the situation in which he found himself. He could not pull out; he could not win. He could only stay and take his punishment. To the cynical, of course, that will be translated into the draftees taking *their* punishment. But I am convinced that every casualty report stabbed him to the heart. They usually came in at 1 A.M. and every night he awoke at that hour and picked up the phone immediately to call the situation room which had the latest reports. When they were bad, he would come to work the next morning with the features of a haunted man. Sometimes he would pass old friends without even an eyeblink of recognition. He was not seeing them because his eyes were focused instead on rice paddies in Vietnam.

I will never share the conviction of the left wing that he deliberately precipitated the war. It is based to a considerable extent on the revelations that came later as to the Gulf of Tonkin episode. Subsequent research disclosed that it was highly unlikely that any torpedoes had been fired at the American vessel. But that is subsequent research. I was in the White House — still press secretary — the night of the retaliatory strike and I know I and my colleagues were all convinced that the crisis was real. If it was a put-up job, this was a fact known only to the president and two or three other people, and while he was a good actor, he was not that good. Furthermore, such a plot would, of necessity, have included Secretary of Defense Robert S. McNamara, and I do not think he would have been a party to such a scheme.

There is no doubt in my mind *now* that the Gulf of Tonkin action was a mistake — at best an overreaction; at worst a colossal blunder. But in my judgment, it is the kind of mistake that is inherent in government. It was a direct result of one of the worst problems in the White House — the all-too-frequent necessity of making crucial

decisions in a crisis when the information is *never* adequate. It is
astonishing to me that this simple truism is so little understood. By
their very nature, crises arise unexpectedly and must be handled on
the spot. The only people who really know what is happening are too
busy coping with events to send more than fragmentary messages
back to Washington. Later, of course, researchers who are not forced
to follow up their conclusions with action enter the scene and, to
them, everything looks quite different. There is enough time to ask
probing questions — and to get answers to them; to distinguish fine
shades of meaning, and to determine their impact. It seems to me
very clear that what happened in regard to the American vessel was
that the skipper was on the bridge — where he ought to be — rather
than down in the cabin composing careful messages to the Pentagon.
After all, there was a chance that his ship was under attack and he
could not desert his command post.

The use that Lyndon Johnson made of the Gulf of Tonkin resolution
was another matter altogether. When he presented the text to the
congressional leaders the night of the retaliation, there was no doubt
that he left in their minds the unmistakable impression that it would
be used only in connection with the specific incident. It was presented to Congress in those terms and approved with that understanding. To use it later as a blanket justification for prosecuting the
war was disingenuous, to say the least. Most of the so-called lies he is
alleged to have told about Vietnam actually amounted to nothing but
excessive optimism and a refusal to face ugly facts. In this instance,
something much more serious is at stake. I suspect he may have
meant what he said the night that he met the congressional leaders
and later rearranged the facts in his own mind to fit the later interpretations. He was capable of such self-deception.

The trouble was that Johnson himself became a victim of the Gulf of
Tonkin Resolution. It froze him into a totally uncompromising position where he had no alternative — or thought he had no alternative
— to feeding more and more draftees into the meat grinder. He had
never, in his entire life, learned to confess error, and this quality —
merely amusing or exasperating in a private person — resulted in
cosmic tragedy for a president. He had to prove that he had been
right all along. And this meant that he had to do more of what he had
been doing despite the demonstrable failure of his Vietnam policies.
Even a change of heart by McNamara, who had been his strongest
supporter both in policy and in action, did not alter his determina-

tion.

It was Clark Clifford who finally found the way out — Clark Clifford who knows more about presidents than any other living man simply because he sees them instinctively as the kings that they are. Where intellectuals and politicians had failed, this man succeeded because he combined a high order of intellect with the skill of a crafty palace guerrilla fighter. He knew what the others had not realized — that no president can be argued into changing his mind but that he can be persuaded to change it if he is led to believe that the change was his own idea.

When Clifford was appointed secretary of defense, he brought to the post a fresh outlook. He was not the prisoner of past commitments. This led him to ask some simple questions which had not been asked before. As he later outlined them (in a memo whose publication was never forgiven by LBJ) the first query was whether it was possible to subdue Vietnam without sending American troops across the border to Hanoi. The answer came back in the negative. His next query was an estimate on the resources that would be required for such a venture. The answer that came back made it clear that commitment of the necessary manpower and material resources would impose an intolerable burden. He set out to persuade the president to snatch for any deal that was possible.

It was an awe-inspiring performance. For some reason that has never been clear to me, I was pulled back into the White House (reluctant to return but incapable of saying "no" to a president) during the final year of Johnson's term. During the first week, I attended a meeting of the Cabinet at which Clifford had been assigned to brief everyone else on Vietnam. He began by ostentatiously removing his watch from his wrist and propping it up on the table before his eyes "so I will not, inadvertently, overstep my allotted seven minutes." He then spoke for twenty-four minutes (I always time people who try such stunts) in low-pitched soothing tones using the dry-as-dust language of a Dickensian lawyer. He then glanced at his watch and said: "I see that I have come to the end of my seven minutes and fortunately it coincides with the end of my report." It was not until later that I realized the full import of what he had said. His words were soporific — so much so that I doubt whether anyone really followed what he was saying. I did. And when I thought through the words, I discovered that he had marshalled every conceivable argument for getting out without actually saying so. It had been virtually a subliminal message.

Lyndon Johnson later denied heatedly that Clifford played any real role in the unexpected decision to bring the Viet Cong and the North Vietnamese to the bargaining table in Paris. Frankly, I could not take his protestations seriously. I believe he just became angered because Clifford published a memorandum outlining his own intellectual processes and thereby (in LBJ's reckoning) asserting a claim to some credit. This was an "offense" which Johnson could not brook. Whether for good or for bad, Clifford changed the course of U.S. policy. I doubt whether the decision actually changed history as there was nothing before us but defeat in Vietnam anyway. Furthermore, the fighting did not end at the conference table in Paris. There was still time to go before the final debacle and the war did end in complete North Vietnamese victory.

As for Johnson's personal fortunes, his change of heart (he denied that it was a change of heart but I do not believe anyone took the denial seriously) came too late to affect his place in history. No matter how much can be chalked up to his credit, he is irrevocably attached to the war. He had feared that the impact upon his historic image would be disastrous. Unfortunately, this was one prophecy which may well be valid.

16

The Aftermath

Were this history or biography, I would have to follow Lyndon B. Johnson to his grave before closing the book. What I am writing, however, falls into neither category. The book ends where LBJ's life really ended — his exit from the presidency. What came afterward is merely of secondary interest to anyone except the small entourage that are attempting — through the library — to make him into something he never was.

My knowledge of the post-presidency period is meager at best. A few tales filtered through of a rather dreary sexual liaison and I learned, through the newspapers, of his break with Mel Winters and A.W. Moursund — the two men I had thought would be his friends to the grave. On one occasion, he visited Washington and made a defense of his career at a meeting of the *Washington Post* Editorial Board, which ended with all the participants rising to their feet and cheering him wildly. But we were not on speaking terms.

Nevertheless, the post-presidential years do not interest me. They must have been hell for his family and for the few staff members who were forced to be close to him. I do not believe the stories about his tranquility. He had spent a lifetime at the eye of the hurricane and I do not think he was enough of a philosopher to adjust to life without power. He was fond of saying that he was "just a country boy." The statement — however inadequate as a description — was true but he never answered the question of whether he enjoyed being a country boy. The ranch was close to him because it gave him a sense of identity. It was his tie to the past and his assurance that there really was a Lyndon B. Johnson. His self-painted portrait of a cattleman tending his herds, however, was difficult to accept with a straight face. He *did* know something about cattle but he "tended" them from a Lincoln Continental with a chest full of ice and a case of scotch and soda in the back seat.

It might have helped him psychologically had he felt some kinship with the Texas mythology so carefully drilled in the children in the state while still in grammar school. He had been accorded that kind of an education but somehow it did not take. The past had no hold on him unless he could relate it to himself or his family. He knew about the Alamo because his father had been responsible for the act that preserved it as a shrine. He knew about the battle of San Jacinto because one of his ancestors had been present. His mother saw to it that he was kept aware of the connection between his great grand-father and Sam Houston. But that was about the limit of his knowl-edge, and even here he was vague.

Once I wrote a speech for him to deliver at some historical society. He read it and called me immediately to give him an explanation of what had happened at Goliad and Washington-on-the-Brazos. I had not known myself until I looked up some dates prior to writing the speech, but I was not a Texan. I had the same reaction as though an Irish nationalist had asked me what happened at the Boyne and Drogheda. This does not mean there was nothing of Texas in him. He was shaped by Texas and the hill country. But it was modern Texas and he had to be briefed with care before talking to an interviewer or an audience of Texas buffs on the days of the pioneers.

One factor which tended to increase his isolation from his sur-roundings was his peculiar status as a politician who was *from* Texas but not truly *in* Texas. His political career had been spent on the national scene, and while at one time he had built a powerful organi-zation within the state, its sole purpose was to sustain him in Washington. His one, whole-hearted foray into the internal politics of Texas had involved a battle with Governor Allan Shivers in 1956 for control of the Democratic delegation *to the national convention* in

1956. This was not an episode that produced old cronies who could gather around him in his declining years and give him a sense of community and of battles past.

Actually, Lyndon Johnson and Texas politics had never been truly compatible. The local politics of the state were passionate, Byzantine, and highly ideological. Conservatives regarded themselves as members of Gideon's army battling the righteous cause of the Lord. Liberals thought of themselves as the last stand of idealism battling a sea of fraud and corruption. Neither could regard the other side in any terms other than venality, and the liberals — probably because they were so small in number — acted as though they were an underground movement. Both sides constructed wild myths and wrote histories of their battles with each other which they considered epics on the scale of the Iliad or the Odyssey but which always seemed to me to be merely tiresome.

To both sides, Lyndon Johnson was the devil incarnate. The conservatives thought of him as a man who had been tarnished by Walter Reuther and Franklin Delano Roosevelt and the liberals as a renegade who trafficked with the evils of reaction. Some of them had some sense, but in the superheated political atmosphere of Texas in the 1950s, it was dangerous to reveal that fact. What is important here is that the political war within the state left LBJ with very few local friends.

Many men in his situation could have found some consolation in organized religion. He could not do so during the days that I knew him and it is unlikely that he changed. He *sought* peace in the church but he could never find it because he was not sure just what it was. Most of his life was spent in "shopping around" different denominations on Sundays. He enjoyed the rituals of the Roman Catholic church, and his night spent with Luci Baines' "little monks" in prayer during the war in Vietnam has become a part of Washington folklore. But he confided to me that "the Catholics and you Episcopalians are hard on the knees."

On one occasion, he and I attended a mass together in the Episcopal church in Fredericksburg — fifteen miles from his ranch. We knelt together at the communion rail and just as the priest started toward me to administer the Host, I felt a nudging in my side. He was handing me a new poll showing an increasing lead over Goldwater in the 1964 campaign. My first reaction was one of anger. But then the humor of the situation struck me and I relaxed — choking back a laugh. It was not really an irreverent act; merely a sharing with God of the things that belong to Caesar. I doubt whether the Almighty was harsh with him for following his instincts.

Much has been made of his close friendship with Billy Graham. I will never be certain of the depth of religious feelings involved, although I am not really cynical about it. But I do know that he had great admiration for Billy's ability to set an audience afire. Johnson's stump oratory style was definitely "Baptist preacher" and his eyes glowed whenever he heard a pastor rip off a fire-and-brimstone sermon. He also understood the politics of religion and moved every-thing he could to load the Equal Employment Opportunity Commis-sion with Baptists when President Kennedy designated him as chairman. He reasoned that the worst problems were in regions where they were predominant and that it was among them that he could do the best missionary work.

What probably contributed the most to his loneliness was a lifetime in which everything he did was designed to achieve a goal. He was not interested in anything for the sake of itself or in people in terms of their backgrounds. To him, nothing was to be studied except for tactical reasons. When I first went to work for him, I told him about my Socialist background as I did not think it fair to have something like that sprung upon him by a conservative constituent. He discov-ered quickly that this gave him some access to a few labor leaders and that was the extent of his curiosity. He never once tried to find out what had made me a Socialist or what had led me to renounce Marxism or what life was like on the city streets of Chicago in the twenties and the thirties. In fact, the only time he ever mentioned my background was in a telephone conservation with a member of the House of Representatives who also had an ex-Socialist working for him. The two men were trying to get together on an incredibly complicated bill — which neither understood — on labor-management relations in the construction industry. LBJ finally roared into the phone: "You send your Socialist over to negotiate with my Socialist and we'll let them settle it."

A life of action was entirely adequate as long as he had been plunged in the continuing struggle. But once he had left the arena, he was lost. There was nothing really sustaining in his relations with the community; his brother (with whom he had not been on speaking terms anyway) had died; he could not relate to religion; there was very little that he enjoyed doing just for the sake of doing it. There was nothing left except a "busy-busy" life with the library and various foundations, and he was not the man for such activity. To really enjoy the season of his decline, he would have had to change a personality that had been built up over a lifetime.

I doubt whether he changed very much in the last few years. There were a few key traits to his personality and it is unlikely that he shed them. As a human being, he was a miserable person — a bully, sadist, lout, and egotist. He had no sense of loyalty (despite his protestations that it was the quality he valued above all others) and he enjoyed tormenting those who had done the most for him. He seemed to take a special delight in humiliating those who had cast in their lot with him. It may well be that this was the result of a form of self-loathing in which he concluded that there had to be something wrong with anyone who would associate with him.

Nevertheless, he was capable of inspiring strong attachments even with people who knew him for what he was. Part of this was bemusement over the sheer size of his pettiness; part of it a mistaken belief that "he didn't mean for true more than half what he said." Even today, I can still feel a certain affection for him regardless of the agony of some of my memories.

In retrospect, I realize that his loutishness was not of the "nature boy" variety. It was customary for his staff to excuse his deplorable manners and his barnyard speech on "the simple ways of a man who was born and lives close to the soil." That was incredible nonsense. Most of his adult life was spent in Washington, D.C., which is not exactly the hookworm and pellagra belt. His lapses from civilized conduct were deliberate and usually intended to subordinate someone else to his will. He did disgusting things because he realized that other people had to pretend that they did not mind. It was his method of bending them to his designs.

Part of the equation was his predilection to be an exhibitionist. He gloried in exposing his body — which was not particularly handsome by normal aesthetic standards — and constantly sought flimsy excuses for doing it. This first emerged in public view with the stories of his "skinny dipping" (swimming naked with other naked men in the White House swimming pool) which he claimed to be a normal pastime among farm boys. This was an explanation which overlooked the fact that he had not been a farm boy in more than four decades. It also overlooked the absence of any water deep enough for swimming in his part of the world when he was a bucolic youth. This exhibitionist tendency was probably the explanation for the famous episode in which he exposed an appendicitis scar to newspaper cameras.

Were there nothing to look at save LBJ's personal relationships with other people, it would be merciful to forget him altogether. But there is much more to look at. He may have been a son of a bitch but he was a colossal son of a bitch. By sheer size alone he would dominate any landscape. And no one could avoid the feeling of an elemental force at work when in his presence. One did not know whether he was an earthquake, a volcano, or a hurricane but one knew that he possessed the force of all three combined and that whatever it was, it might go off at any moment.

One of the more important lapses of the Washington press corps was the assertion that compared with John F. Kennedy he "had no style." I know of no better example of the ovine characteristics of capital journalists. However else Lyndon Johnson might be described, he had "style" in the plain sense of the word — style beside which Jack Kennedy, for all his attractive qualities, faded into the background. When LBJ entered a room, everyone knew it immediately and the people within would divide accordingly. Except for the vice presidential years, he was, at all times, the focal point of action.

At his best, he also possessed the finest quality of a politician. It was a sense of the direction of political power — the forces that were sweeping the masses. He did not merely content himself by getting ahead of those forces. He mastered the art of directing them. He could ride currents of public opinion as could few other men. To his credit, it should be said that he usually tried to ride them in the direction of uplift for the poor and downtrodden.

There is no doubt about his nastiness in dealing with individual human beings. But neither can there be any real doubt about his sincerity in trying to do something for the masses. His feelings for blacks, Chicanos, dirt farmers were not feigned. He felt their plight and suffered with them — as long as they did not get too close.

Of all of his qualities, however, the most important was that he knew how to make our form of government work. That is an art that has been lost since his passing and we are suffering heavily as a result. It was a peculiar quality in that it had its limitations. He was not a man of grand design. His ideas were simplistic and amounted to little more than placing economic floors under wages, farm prices, and business income, plus universal education and medical care and cheap electric power. But he could take ideas from other men and women who were totally incapable of putting them into effect. In his hands, they would be shaped into programs of action. Among our presidents, he should be rated as the master tactician of all times.

The tragedy is that he used that talent to take us into the most disastrous war in our history. I hope that will not be his final epitaph. He was wrong — as usual, the mistake was colossal — and the consequences were tragic. I doubt whether he will be forgiven. But that is not enough to pass judgment on the man. He obviously had qualities which this country needs and it is becoming more apparent with each passing day that our system does not work well without his kind of operation. It is becoming commonplace for me to encounter people who a few years ago were proclaiming their hatred of him and who now are sighing for his return.

I, myself, am glad to get him out of my life at last. I do not believe anyone could be happy around him for any length of time. But I would be very happy to see him back in government — in a position where he could pick up the loose ends as he did in 1952 and in 1963, and weld them into a unified whole. What I would like, of course, would be a Lyndon B. Johnson who was *not* a bastard; who *did* know how to confess the error of Vietnam; but who retained the unifying skill required for the health of the American democracy.

Of course, we are not going to get that. He was a tormented man and while we will never know why he was tormented, we must acknowledge the fact. He was a bundle of contradictions and we will have to accept him the way he was. I only hope we really accept him that way — not a saint and not a demon but still a towering figure on the landscape of American history.